Richard Fleischman

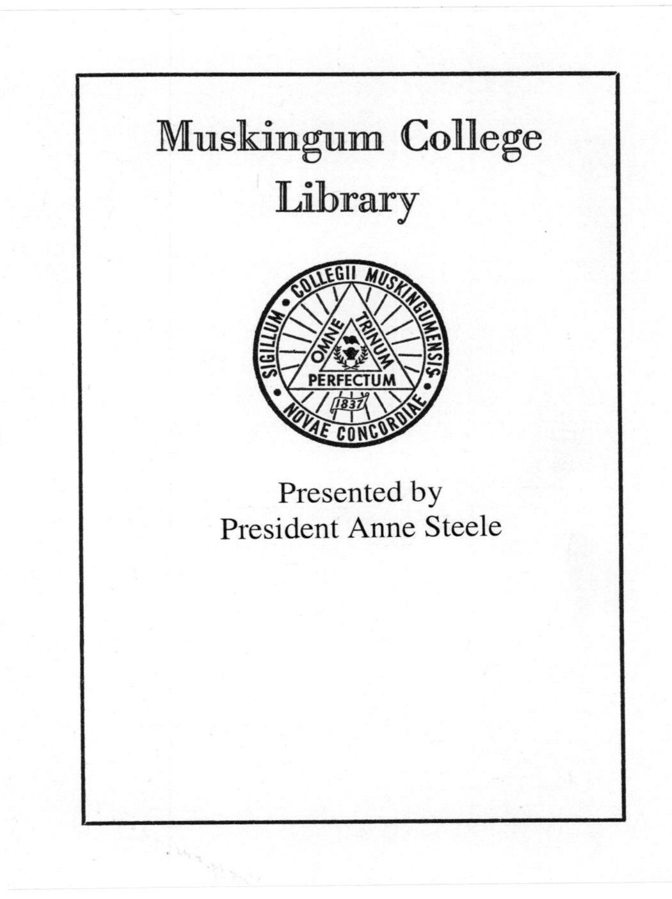

Editorial Director USA
Pierantonio Giacoppo

Chief Editor of Collection
Maurizio Vitta

Publishing Coordinator
Franca Rottola

Graphic design
CREA Studio, Milano

Photographies
Richard Fleischman Archives, Eric Hanson

Translation
Martyn J. Anderson

Colour Separation
Litofilms, Bergamo

Printing
Poligrafiche Bolis, Bergamo

First published June 1996

Printed in Italy
Library of Congress Catalog Card Number:
96 - 076173

ISBN 88-7838-014-8

Richard Fleischman

Spaces to be Shared

Preface *by Richard Fleischman*
Introduction *by Maurizio Vitta*

l'ARCAEDIZIONI

CONTENTS

7 Preface *by Richard Fleischman*
9 Introduction *by Maurizio Vitta*
17 Works
18 Elyra D.C. Gymnasium
22 Holy Family Church
26 Bible Community Church
30 Karunga Mission Church
34 Ontario United Methodist Church
38 St. Edmund Catholic Church
42 Kingsbury Run
44 Pioneer Memorial Church
48 Villa Angela Academy
54 Church of the Covenant and Hallinan Center
58 St. Elizabeth's Catholic Church
62 St. Paschal Baylon Church
68 Bellflower Elementary School
74 Christ the King Lutheran Church
78 Kent State University Memorial Gymnasium Annex
82 ADP
86 Cox Cable
88 Span the Tracks Study, University of Akron
94 Millersburg Church
98 Stow-Monroe Falls High School
104 Community School
106 Ontario-Huron Center
112 Mountainlair Student Union Building
116 Studio of Richard Fleischman Architects
120 College of Engineering Nitschke Hall, University of Toledo
124 North Coast Harbor Developement, Design Guidelines/Master Plan
128 Convention Plaza Hotel Office Retail Complex
132 Cleveland Center for Contemporary Art
136 Ashtabula High School
142 Polymer Science Building University of Akron
148 Human Services and Support Agencies Building, County of Cuyahoga
154 Breezy Bluff Estate
162 Plateau Senior High School Lake Washington School District
166 Ohio Aerospace Institute
174 Cleveland Public Library Memorial, Nottingham Branch
180 Auburn Career Center
184 The Entertainement Wheel
186 Cleveland Convention Center
191 Richard Fleischman Architects, Inc.

Preface

One building standing alone in an open landscape is a work of architecture. This free-standing building, regardless of silhouette or surface architecture, is an object in space, and seldom contributes to urban design. However, organize buildings together, and another art form is possible. Several things begin to happen in the composition; they create what could not be possible for the isolated building. You may have the opportunity to walk through and past the collection of structures; as the path changes direction, new and unusual experiences of an entirely different mass, profile, or facade can occur as a result of an unsuspected or unknown location. Beauty in architecture and cities is largely dependent upon their harmonious and artful relationship to space.

To design urban space as a foreceful display of architectural creativity, and design it so that it can be used and occupied by everyone in a relatively unselfconscious manner, requires a sense of balance not unlike Schopenhauer's description of the beauty that exists in architecture - it occurs only when gravity and support are equal forces.

One can observe the history of the city as a scaffold to which ideologies reflected as architecture and urban design are attached as a dynamic reservoir from which alternative ideological interests emerge or are renewed. It is clear, from the initial development of cities, that people have added, remodeled, and subtracted from their community setting in the most dynamic manner, and the style of architecture had little to do with its success. The architecture of the city is a diverse and often complex text of visual symbols. It has a universal relationship to the city, it is unique because it is unlike other art forms, it is scrutinized in full view, it can neither control nor escape the city's form and boundaries. It can be identified as an art of intervention and the creative relationships that result are integral to its success.
The contextual quality of our cities is a relatively new element that has emerged as a significant component that describes traditional detail and character. It is apparent that new developments with newer techniques and technology of construction can readily create new options with new opportunities. Professionals who employ architectural principles as well as urban design criteria have initiated innovative planning concepts that produce infill solutions while maintaining the historical character of the city.
Good urban design must inspire the use of space and attract people. Unquestionably it is the concentration of buildings and people that give cities their dynamic quality. Urban design may be regarded as a synthetic inventure mapping of physical conditions establishing and exploring areas of the city. It is the further definition of the architecture of space. It is the critical combination of general notions of urbanism and specific concepts. The intent of urban design is to seek a logical and strategic articulation of elements inherent in an exciting condition. Unique to this spatial organization is the invention of walls, streets, public spaces, and building topologies that resolve existing ambiguities in the form of the city.

Richard Fleischman

INTRODUCTION
by Maurizio Vitta

Questions of Method

Richard Fleischman, Senior Partner of Richard Fleischman Architects, Inc., Cleveland (Ohio), referred to Schopenhauer's theories on architecture when reflecting on his own work. "To design urban spaces as a forceful display of architectural creativity", he claimed, "and design it so that it can be used and occupied by everyone in a relatively unselfconscious manner requires a sense of balance not unlike Schopenhauer's description of the beauty that exists in architecture - it occurs only when gravity and support are equal forces".
This allusion to Schopenhauer's thoughts on architecture is such a strange and interesting insight that it deserves to be examined in greater detail. In his most important work, *The World as Will and Representation*, the German philosopher and incurable romantic placed the arts in hierarchical order according to their relation to ideas: in his opinion, the function of great works of art is to encourage aesthetic contemplation. In this sense, architecture (which, by its very nature, is made of matter and "as such cannot be the expression of an Idea") touches "the lowest grades of the will's objectivity. Such Ideas are gravity, cohesion, rigidity, hardness....and along with these, light" (III, § 43). But in architecture "gravity" conflicts with the rules of architectural composition so "the only truly aesthetic purpose of beautiful architecture" is to bring these conflicting forces into balance. Schopenhauer is basically claiming that the force of matter chains architecture to the ground, subjecting it to the laws of utility, but the composition of its parts raises it up, allowing it to break free from the bonds of "will" and aspire to the heights of the representation of an idea.
Schopenhauer did not have as clear a grasp of these matters as Hegel, who sensed the representative force and symbolic or even spiritual nature of architecture. Nevertheless, his image of beauty deriving not from a harmonious blend of form and function (as the exponents of the Modern Movement were later to claim), but from their conflicting relations, constantly recurring and only momentarily resolved, is more pertinent than ever.
It is interesting to note that Fleischman has touched on these questions for methodological rather than aesthetic reasons. He is, in fact, alluding to the deeply problematic and contradictory nature of building, accepting the challenge this poses. "A new building provides the community with more than a new structure", so he claims. "It embodies the essence of an ideology and impels the user towards the future".
This attitude stems from a careful analysis of the state of contemporary architecture as it grapples with the problems of entering a new millennium, but its roots are actually even more deeply entrenched. The bold claims of the Modern Movement have been called into question over the last thirty years or so; and recent history is profoundly scarred by attempts to invent a new approach to architecture capable of expressing the increasing complexity of the world in which we live.

A Thirty-Five-Year-Story

Richard Fleischman Architects, Inc., was first established back in 1961. During this period, the studio has witnessed numerous changes and developments in our society, transformations that first began to make themselves felt back in the late Fifties.
In those days, modern architecture was producing some of its most memorable works: the Seagram Building in New York, designed by Mies van der Rohe, was already an important landmark for many young architects; Frank Lloyd Wright had just completed the

Guggenheim Museum in New York; Eero Saarinen was building the TWA Terminal at Kennedy Airport; Le Corbusier was working on the Carpenter Center for Visual Arts in Cambridge, Massachusetts. All these buildings have left their mark on the history of American architecture.

Each in its own way embodies an entire architectural culture that has reached the peaks of its powers and is supremely confident in both its means and ends. This gradual process of maturation certainly was not without its contradictions, first sensed within the movement itself. Its underlying principles, placing heavy emphasis on the social function of architecture, had been worked out half-a-century ago, but they now needed to be re-examined in light of the dramatic changes that had taken place in western society since the IInd World War. The debate on housing in the United States and, more significantly, the polemics surroundings "monumentalism" provided a revealing insight into the new historical parameters with which architecture now had to come to terms. The issues raised in the construction of certain American embassies showed just what was at stake: architects were now expected to widen their horizons and give material substance to much more complicated values. New concepts were emerging, such as "place" and "communication". We need only examine the embassies built by Edward Durrell Stone in New Delhi, John Johansen in Dublin and Eero Saarinen in London during that period to realise just how complex and far-reaching the concept of "function", so dear to the great masters of modernity, had now become.

Louis Kahn's theories on "monumentalism" and the influence of his work on the rationalist movement (the Richards Medical Research Building in Philadelphia was completed in 1964, a year before the Salk Institute in La Jolla, California) marked the new frontiers of architecture. Kahn's theory that architecture ought to be a "creating of spaces that evoke a feeling of use" was rather confusing, but it allowed debate on architectural form to move on from the dilemma between function and ornament to the more fertile grounds of psychology, memory and aesthetics in general.

Modern architecture was not rejected, it was just revised and projected onto a different plane. During this same period, Paul Rudolph and John Johansen were working on theories of structural disarticulation and drawing up a complex geometrical representation of space, acutely aware of just how indebted they were to the modern movement, but equally determined to break free from the conformism of structural rigour to express the underlying tensions of a society that had changed dramatically over the last few decades.

The question of architectural "image" and its capacity to "represent" social and cultural values was becoming a crucial issue. Robert Venturi's House of Mrs. Venturi in Chestnut Hill, Pennsylvania, caused quite a sensation in 1964, but it really did nothing more than take the issue to its most extreme consequences. On one hand, architecture had lost the normative connotations of old-style rationalism, while on the other, it had taken on global cultural consequences that turned every single building into a web of values and meanings. By the early Sixties, the essentially conflicting nature of the relationship between "form" and "function", "image" and "structure", "aesthetics" and "utility" had come to the fore, just as Schopenhauer had sensed, and had now shifted onto much more treacherous, but also more fertile terrain. The history of architecture over the last thirty-five years had gradually evolved around these issues, driven along by the crisis in modernity and the emergence of "postmodern" consciousness, which, despite a gradual drying-up of its vocabulary and the increasing sterility of the works it produces, is still the guiding force behind contemporary architecture.

Thirty-five Years' Work

Richard Fleischman began his career at a time when the anxieties and unease surrounding architecture were bringing the rationalist period to a close and opening up a new cycle much more conscious of epoque-making changes, but still incapable of providing an effective working model. The new issues emerging were still riddled with problems: the geometric space invoked by architecture in the early twentieth century was gradually giving way to historical space in a web of memories and experiences; functionalism no longer held the key to the social issues underpinning architecture; rapid technological progress favoured non-Cartesian design criteria that reflected the growing complexity of contemporary culture in the actual buildings they produced.

Fleischman managed to glean the most positive aspects from this critical state of affairs. By introducing patient research, carefully gauged pragmatism and a concern for the natural-human environment in place of certain knowledge, cultural dogmas and theoretical models, he took full advantage of the formal freedom made possible by the gradual decline in ideologies, skillfully exploiting the opportunities provided by continual improvements in building technology. He refused to yield to either the temptation of form as pure image or technology as pure language. He realised from the very start that each separate architectural project is an experience in itself and not the embodiment of some abstract design theory. But he also sensed that they are also the result of patiently piecing together conflicting elements.

This is the key to the studio's unfaltering coherency over all these years. The same underlying principles can be traced through every single project by Richard Fleischman Architects. As the history of architecture has gradually splintered into a myriad of separate episodes over recent decades, in which the architect's personality has taken precedence over all-embracing cultural theories, Fleischman has remained faithful to the notion of architecture as incessant research in which innovation is counterbalanced by powerful bonds with the physical, historical and anthropical environment. For Fleischman architecture must be guided by both structural considerations and practical requirements.

These are the same ideas that emerged from the crisis in rationalism, but without the characteristic over-indulgence of personal poetics. It is no coincidence that the most frequently arising image in Fleischman's own thoughts is the mosaic. "Our approach is like an intricate mosaic", so he writes. In it "the mortar binding the individual pieces is a mix of collaboration and patience. Essentially, our design process represents an intense investigation of complex problems that cannot be approached with predetermined solutions. Instead, we pull into the process more mosaic pieces - a multitude of considerations". The image of the mosaic illustrates the concept of complexity, that frequently looms up menacingly over contemporary design, but softens it down and brings it back to an ordinary dimension of day-to-day business. It embodies an awareness that architecture is not the result of some sort of *coincidentia oppositorum*, but a battle between conflicting forces which Fleischman himself lists as ranging from the "needs expressed by the client and by future users of the spaces" to "environmental conditions and energy conservation", "funding capabilities and constraints" and "special site and context considerations". A blend of healthy pragmatism, professional conscientiousness and contemporary culture permeates all these concepts. This is confirmed by the underlying philosophy behind the studio: "it is our imagination, teamed with an understanding of technology, that allows us to anticipate change and to channel our intellectual resources in positive directions". "Conflict", taken as the driving force behind architecture, is the philosophical thread running through these reflections on architecture and design.

Faith, Science, Culture

Richard Fleischman Architects have a whole range of architectural and town-planning projects on their curriculum. But, generally speaking, they have shown a marked propensity for either places of worship or education facilities (schools, museums, art galleries) and science buildings. The sheer scope of these two categories of buildings inevitably divides them into two homogeneous design categories, for each of which every individual project represents a different variation on the same theme. Not that these projects are the fruits of the same, constantly recurring approach, since each conforms to its own design criteria. Yet space constructed for either religious or scientific purposes must, in some way, provide room for and mirror behavioural patterns, states of mind, activities and expectations which are embodied in well defined and codified rituals; and this means that architecture must adapt to a pre-established functional scheme. This problematic contrast between the relative inflexibility of project requirements and the relative autonomy of architecture is, of course, the point of departure and driving force behind every new project. But it inevitably takes on a decidedly dramatic tone when it comes to designing places of worship or premises for scientific research and its diffusion. Viewed in abstract synthesis, the two groups may instantly be pigeonholed into the categories of faith and reason: reciprocally irreconcilable, as we all know. Architecture, in turn, has its own pair of equally inflexible binary oppositions to set against these categories, or in other words imagination and calculation.
Fleischman has always been well aware of architecture's primary task, as well as its potential and limitations. He knows that designing a church means giving physical form, space and concrete essence to liturgy and its symbolic rituals, just as designing a scientific institute or home for the arts means organising layouts, rooms and services according to the conceptual logic that governs scientific research. Discretion has always been the key to his own particular approach to these technical constraints or, in a manner of speaking, careful attention to the activities that will take place in the building once completed. Intimate knowledge of the client's requirements is for Fleischman something more than just professional ethics: it is a design principle embodied in attention to detail. It is no coincidence that the studio has even designed the stained glass windows of certain churches such as St. Martin's in Tours, the first in a series of churches.
In contrast, the spaces and structures of a construction like the Ohio Aerospace Institute are designed to correspond perfectly to the educational/scientific purposes of the client. In this case, implicit architectural symbolism is expressed through a form of technology designed to help concentration and encourage research, and through a type of transparency that allows light to imbue the structures and colour relations with the kind of drive typical of man's adventure in space. Of course, this attitude runs through all the work carried out by Richard Fleischman Architects. The principle of directly confronting the either openly avowed or gently alluded to specifications underpinning an architectural design is a constant in both projects for private houses and major urban development schemes. This form of confrontation is obviously more evident in those projects in which the building's symbolic or representative connotations are explicitly intended to be an end in themselves. In those cases where an architectural structure needs to be translated into a language for communicating precise messages through the silent eloquence of forms, the search for aesthetic solutions serves an intrinsically functional purpose. Even Schopenhauer realised this when he claimed that "the great merit of architecture" consists in pursuing aesthetic ends, but subordinating them if necessary to functional criteria, "rightly judging what kind of architectural-aesthetic beauty is most appropriate and fitting for a temple, for a palace, for an arsenal and so forth".

Place and Environment

The most authentic strain of modern rationalism attempted to resolve the conflict between interior and exterior, urban structure and individual space that lies at the very heart of contemporary architectural debate. Unfortunately, the results were rather disappointing. As rationalism degenerated into mere style without ever really developing into the kind of social ideology that Gropius had hoped for, the exterior appearance of buildings became the primary design criterion mechanically dictating the arrangement of interior space. This explains why postmodernism subsequently reacted along two distinct lines: on one hand, it set out to restore expressive qualities to building design through interaction with the surrounding context and location; on the other, it attempted to free industrial design - particularly home furnishing - from the cold design criteria of functionalism, in order to accommodate the user's emotional/temperamental requirements.
As industrial design opened up its gates to psychology, architecture was rediscovering the values of history, memory and the environment. The crisis in the Modern Movement stemmed from a suspicion that the "internationalism" of design was degenerating into an inexpressive atopia, tending to reduce architectural projects to isolated episodes cut off from their surroundings and bereft of any genuinely desirable cultural or social values. As we have seen, this problem had already been touched upon in architectural debate in the early Sixties; but it took another decade before it could be approached with any real awareness of all its implications.
Richard Fleischman did not wait for the reactionary drive of postmodernism to reflect on the significance of "place" and "context" in architecture. He immediately felt totally at ease with these concepts, and although at the beginning he might not have been fully aware of their cultural implications, he was convinced that they deserved their own rightful place in architectural design. The projects from his early career - mainly schools or churches buildings - work along two main lines: architectural designs mirroring the characteristic features of local buildings, and more careful attention than ever to spatial integration into the physical environment. The exteriors of Fleischman's churches and schools seem to cling instinctively to their site locations thanks to their low, flat structures, wide triangular facades and simple architectural forms reminiscent of factory buildings - all of which are characteristic features of spontaneous American architecture, especially in the wide open spaces of the inland states. The question of "regionalism", which is currently being hotly debated in most architectural circles, had already been broached and even resolved in these buildings. Yet the actual image projected by these places - a way of being, more than a way of living - has the same immediacy and intensity as Grant Wood's paintings. If anything architecture is expected to trace the path of this gradually evolving image. In Fleischman's buildings it is translated into a contemporary idiom without losing any of its vibrant sense of tradition.
The way these structures interact with the physical environment and blend in like natural extensions to the landscape seems to be a logical consequence of this tightly knit bond with history. More than mere respect for nature, it is a firm belief that architecture, as an expression of society, must constantly seek to create a balance between nature and artifact. These particular projects by Fleischman clearly glean the legacy of rationalism, projecting it into the present so that it can be measured up against a growing awareness of a new set of problems facing architecture. In these buildings, designed to smoothly (but intensely) interact with the wide open spaces in which they are located, architectural "space" is transformed into "place" to the extent in which it succeeds in counterbalancing the dynamic/chronological dimension of history with the stabilising, material forces of nature.

Town Planning

The question of interaction between place and architecture is reproposed, but from a different angle, in inner-cities. The city is the architectural place par excellence and, as such, it is an instance of total identification between these two separate dimensions. This means that architects are inevitably faced with an entirely new set of problems, particularly at a time like ours when the urban environment has expanded to form the very foundations of human existence. Town-planning has totally transformed conventional relations between architecture and its surroundings. An artifact tends to allow itself to be absorbed by nature so as to assimilate its intrinsic vitality without harming the environment. The roles are reversed with buildings and cities, as architecture attempts to impose itself on its surrounding context in the form of a dominant "landmark". The dynamic, transformative powers of each new building knit into the urban fabric inevitably alter the existing equilibrium. The apparent violence of this act is not perceived as such by the city, which, on the contrary, feeds off a transformative process that lies at the very roots of its history. A variety of design criteria associated with various different schools of thought may be derived from this premise. The Modern Movement interpreted town-planning as an inexhaustible source of new architectural forms; postmodernism reacted by reverting back to the key historical features of the city and projecting them into the present. In any case, architecture and the city are treated on the same level, as two sides of the same coin. Richard Fleischman has paid careful attention to this aspect of his work. He firmly believes that the organisation of a group of buildings is a different form of art from the design of one single building. He sees the city as an active, living organism whose feverish activity must be traced out by architecture: architectural design is responsible for physically embodying the social function of this place of innovation and change.
Fleischman's urban development schemes and projects for entire housing estates and residential/conference centres all stem from these considerations, which are then developed into a more extensive scheme encompassing such factors as traffic flows, connections and economic prospects. However, as soon as the city becomes the focus of his work, his architecture changes appearance.
Faced, in his town-planning work, with a totally built environment submerged in artificial nature and an historical context that both lie entirely within its bounds, his architecture seems to enjoy the kind of freedom and daring which, elsewhere, are rather dampened by their direct interaction with other cultural categories. This provides a clearer insight into the underlying features of Fleischman's approach to design: his original allegiance to critical rationalism is still firmly intact; but at the same time we can sense the careful scrutiny with which he has traced the developments in architecture during the late XXth century. Above all, there is an underlying sense of architectural balance and wisdom that have enabled him to treat stylistic and technological innovations with great measure and discretion.
This has kept Fleischman well away from flights of aesthetic fancy and the kind of excessive technicalism that are so commonplace on the contemporary architectural scene. He has always adhered to the imperative of seeking to provide a social/cultural service.

Towards the XXIst Century

These considerations take us back to the underlying premise behind Richard Fleischman's work, his awareness of the fact that architecture derives from a battle between conflicting forces. He knows that the right balance between these forces lies in the actual act of construction and not pure theory. This also takes us back to the question of the relations between the architect's intentions and the constraints and guidelines dictated by society in general and architectural culture in particular. The history of architecture over the last fifty years has been a melting pot of tumultuous events. The proclamation and then dissolution of various general theories, mainly hinging around a simple style or reduced to expressions of personal taste, has highlighted not so much architecture's struggle to overcome the crisis in rationalism, as the difficulties experienced by a whole society - and, consequently, an entire culture - in providing a coherent solution to the demands of the age in which we live.
Architects - leading figures in a mass society seeking alternative living conditions and hence new spatial layouts - are faced with the task of designing the primary environment of community life in our age, or in other words the cityscape, and at the same time of working out a balance between the natural and historical environments - another set of indispensable binary oppositions at the end of the millennium. Richard Fleischman witnessed all this from the very beginning; he belongs to a generation of architects who, although educated in the shadow of mature rationalism, were already acutely aware of its decline in the face of new forms of reality. During his career he personally experienced all the shocks, excitement and contradictions inherent in a culture desperately seeking more stable balances. Yet, despite being fully aware of working in the uncertainty of a constantly evolving context, he has resisted the allure of various theories and styles in the firm belief that architecture derives, above all, from the conflict and dialogue inherent in every new project. In his opinion, architecture must confront technological progress with changes in social requirements, the specific demands of individual clients, the historical-physical state of the surrounding environment, and the range of possible projections envisaged in the future. The outcome of this confrontation between conflicting forces must be "good architecture", the same target the great masters of early this century set themselves and which remains, despite all the changes that have taken place, the ultimate purpose of design. Fleischman's approach is inspired by the severity and modesty of a professional approach whose roots are entrenched deep in the past. Yet he certainly is not lacking in levelheaded ambition: "'No matter what the style'", so he writes, "the final 'defined space' will be timeless. Good architecture maintains a consistent quality and image, which represents not only a network of artistic and functional spaces, but a powerful commitment to great design". Bearing this in mind, Richard Fleischman Architects are entitled to weigh up their concrete achievements in positive terms: "With almost 40 years of practice and hundreds of completed projects throughout the United States, ranging from simple building renovations to complex mixed-use developments, many of which have received national or regional awards, our work may be classed as meeting a demand for excellence. The word that best describes the buildings and plans designed by Richard Fleischman Architects, Inc., is 'intense'. Our projects are distinctly different from one another, each reflective of its own program, site, design constraints and client expectations. Where some of our designs have been applauded for being 'dignified', 'restrained' or 'sensitive to context', a few others have earned the tag 'innovative', 'daring' or 'cutting edge'". This pride in their work is quite justified, as is their serene confidence in the fact that this wealth of experience and architectural expertise will enable them to face the challenges of the XXIst century with quiet resolve.

Works

ELYRIA D.C. GYMNASIUM
Elyria, Ohio
1964

A comparison between the efficient use of shape defined by a square as against an oval determined the shape of the gymnasium. The design analysis suggested two levels consisting of a playing court for physical education and competitive sports, as well as a level for auxiliary gymnasium functions. When the bleachers are expanded, the entire facility can become a spectator center seating 3,500. Additional capacity on the playing floor can accommodate auditorium seating for 4,500.

The space can also, on occasion, provide for a dining facility since the large oval is contiguous with the kitchen facility. A lower level houses the locker and shower rooms along with team rooms. The addition is connected with the existing school corridor system providing convenient access for students participating in the physical education program, and is adjacent to the main lobby to provide access for people involved in all spectator sports and assemblies.

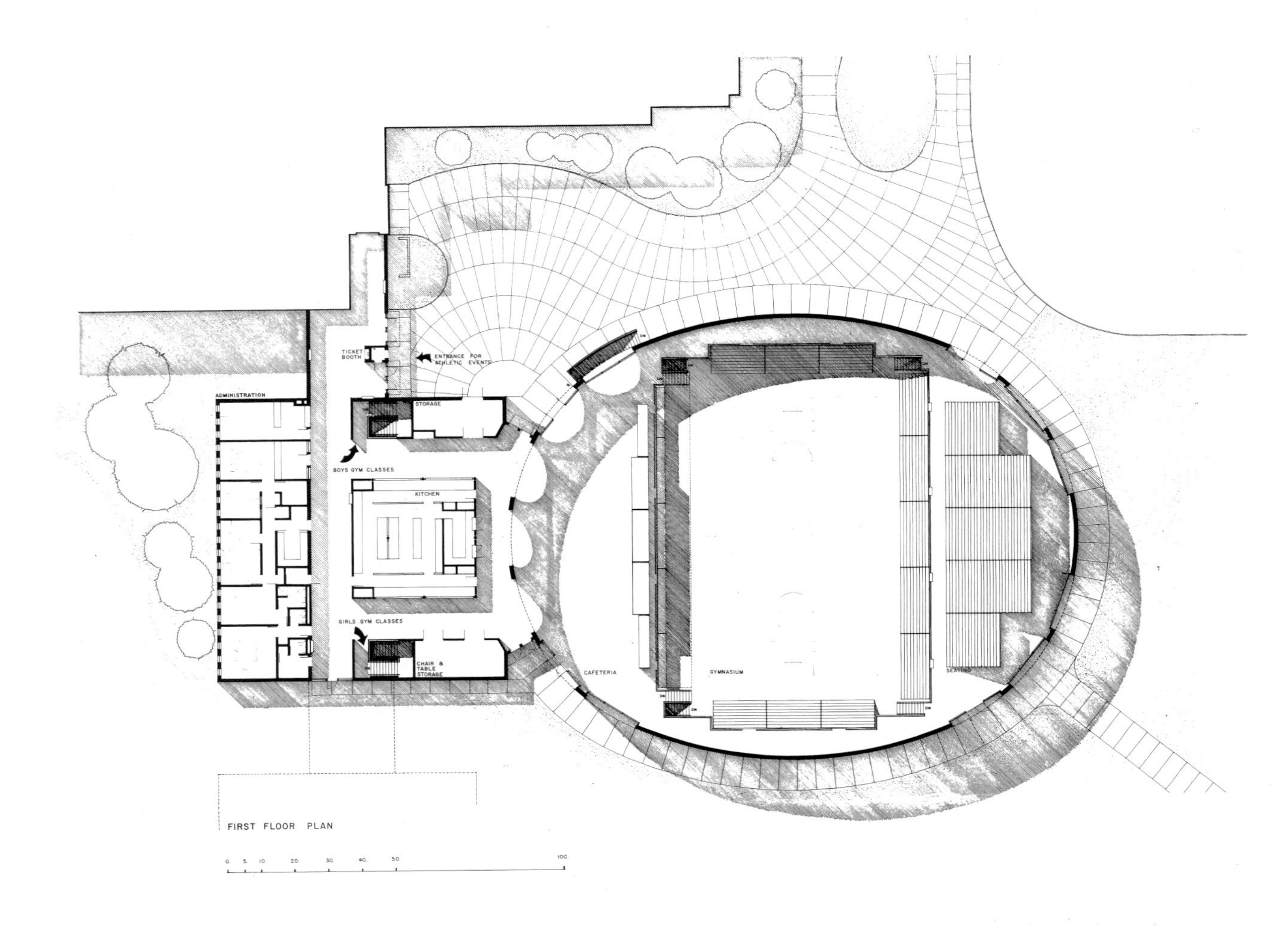

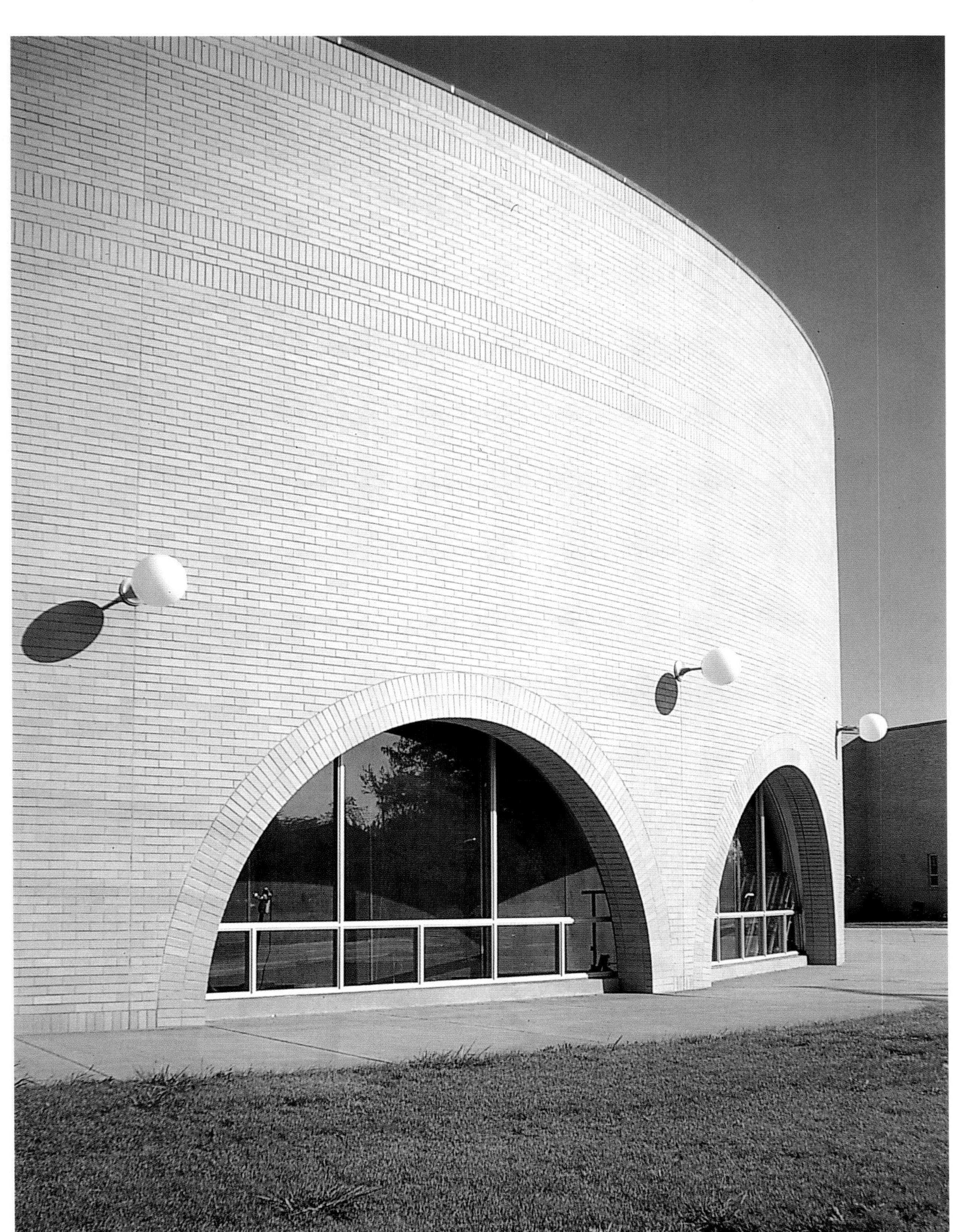

Partial view on the gymnasium side.
Opposite page, plan of the first floor of the complex.

Top of page, plan of the gymnasium showing the layout of the stands and, bottom of page, plan of the first-floor services.

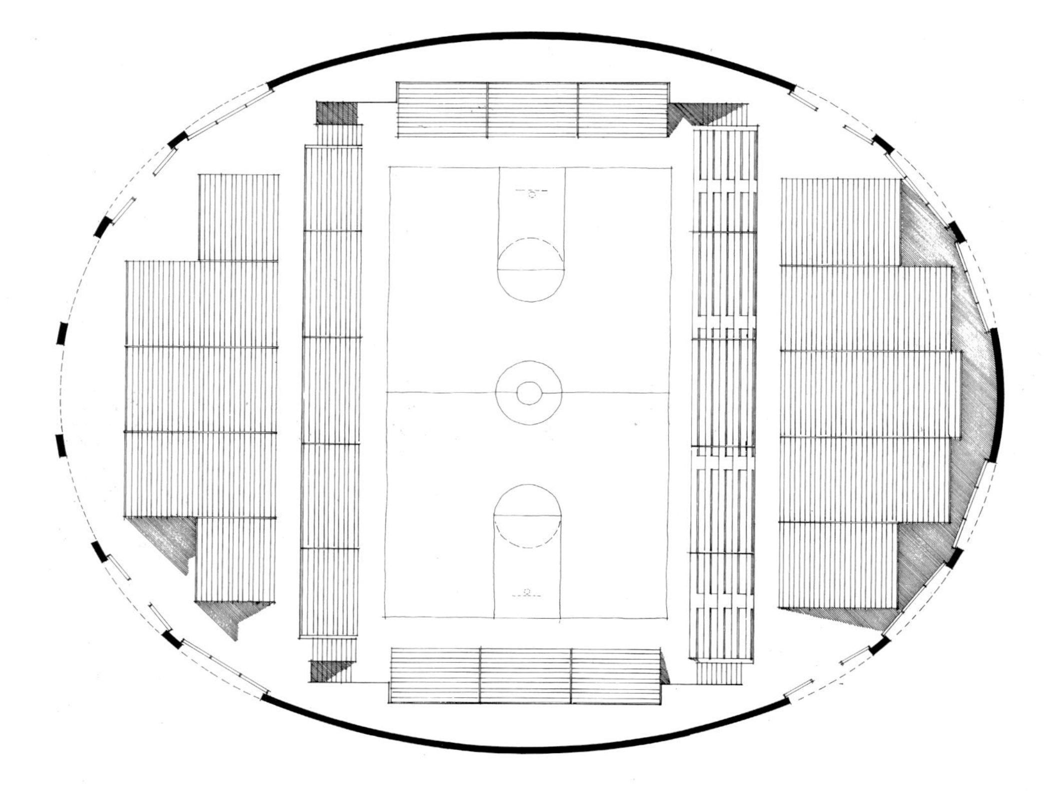

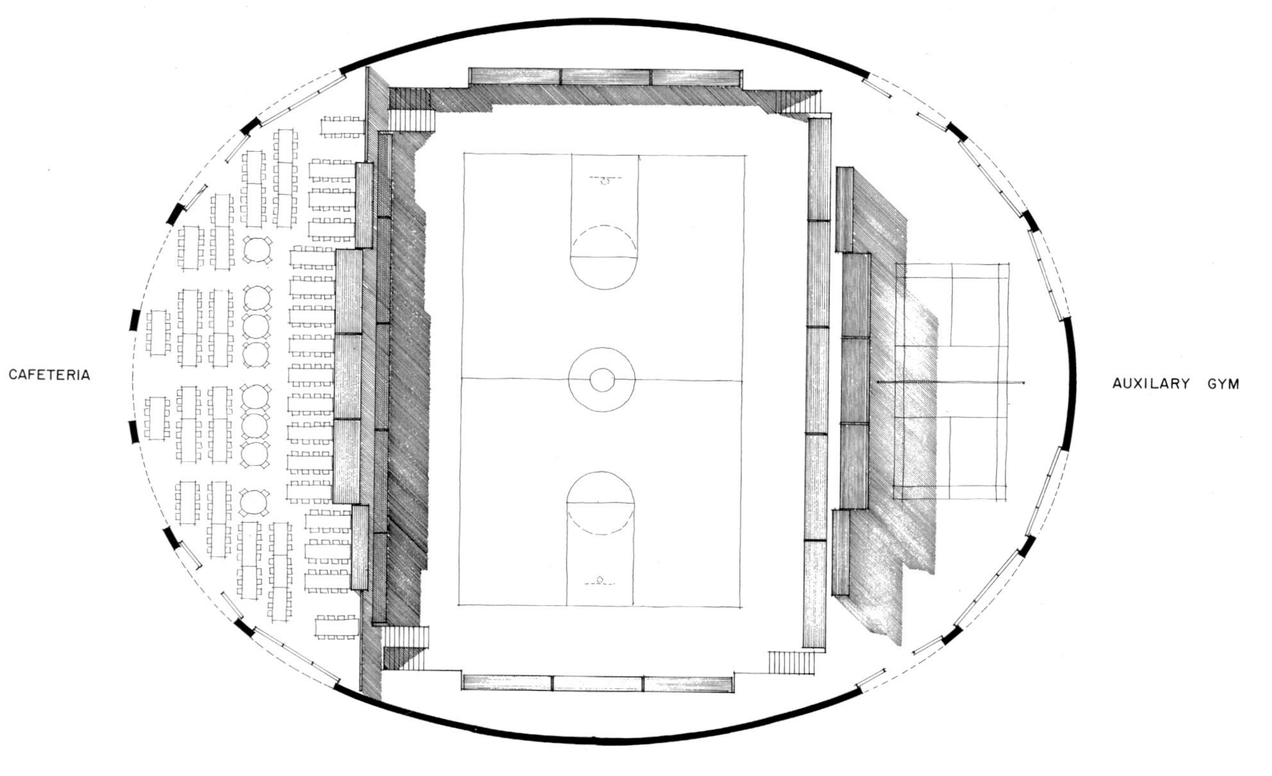

Top of page, exterior view of the main building; bottom of page, partial view of the gymnasium.

HOLY FAMILY CHURCH
Parma, Ohio
1965

The purpose of a Catholic Church Building is to provide a place where people can assemble to conduct the liturgical life of the Church.
The congregation assembles for the primary purpose of worshipping God. In the Catholic Church, the supreme act of worship is Mass.
This Church has been designed to incorporate the concept of liturgical form and symbolism in its visual, auditory and acoustic space. All the elements of liturgy are related to the main axis of the Church. The Baptistery acts as a gateway leading through to the Sanctuary. Both the interior and exterior of the Shrines and Confessionals are related to this main axis. The various segments have different radii, developing undulating planes on both the exterior and interior. Each segment of the circle, designed to symbolize an interior function, is reflected on the exterior. The Church seats 1350 in the Nave, with seating room for 120 in the balcony and additional space for another 50 in the two Mothers' Rooms.
The curved walls are made of poured-in-place concrete using specially designed forms and using a carefully specified concrete mix and aggregate. A Wyandotte White Limestone was chosen for the aggregate. All of the exposed concrete is bush hammered. The interior finish features terrazzo floors and plaster walls with an acoustical plaster ceiling. The interior of the Church is completely mechanically ventilated and, if need be in the future, can be air conditioned.

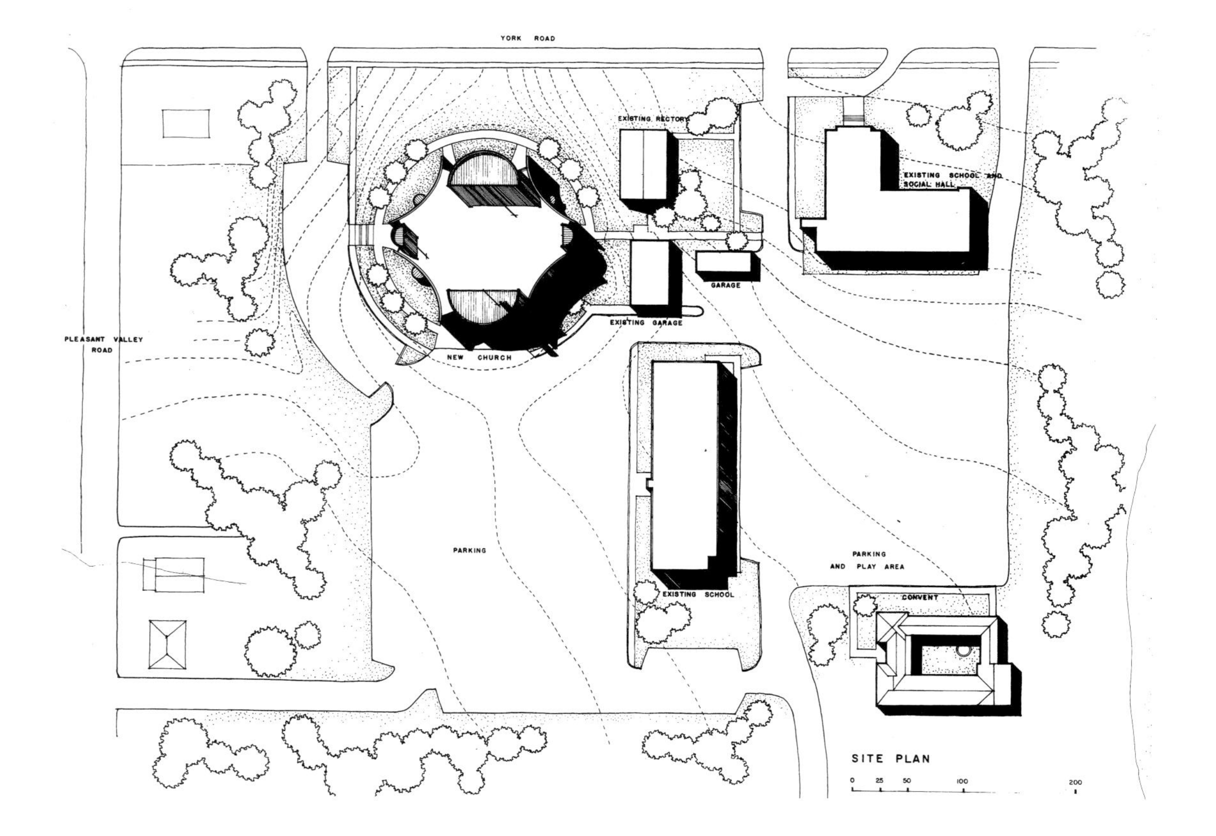

A picture of the church
showing its convex and
concave interplay of surfaces
and volumes.
Opposite page, site plan.

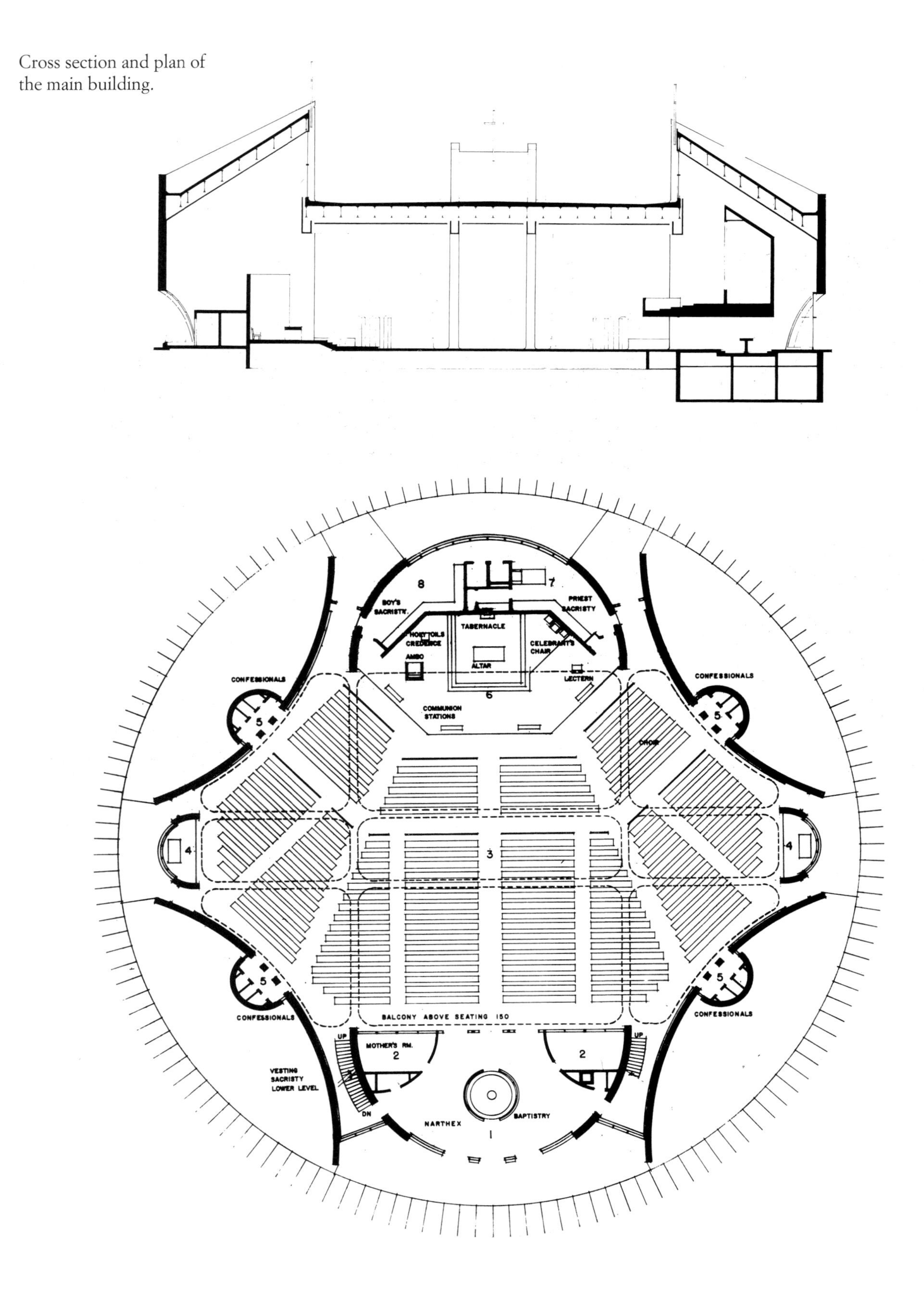

Cross section and plan of the main building.

Interior of the church with its multi-faced oak-wood wall, marble altar and terrazzo floor.

BIBLE COMMUNITY CHURCH
Mentor, Ohio
1965

The program analysis of Bible Community Church suggested a unique arrangement of space designed to provide flexible areas for a congregation actively involved in worship, fellowship and education on Sundays, and other events during the week.
A traditional sanctuary obviously would not provide the type of flexibility required. It soon became apparent that a central core space was needed that could be expanded to double the seating capacity for worship. It was also decided to build an education area with room for 1000 members which, if need be, could later be extended to accommodate up to 1200. The seashell-shaped structure focuses on the center of the circle without destroying visual access to the worship and education areas.
The unpainted concrete block walls stand in stark contrast to the cedar sliding used on the exterior between the bearing walls of the classrooms.

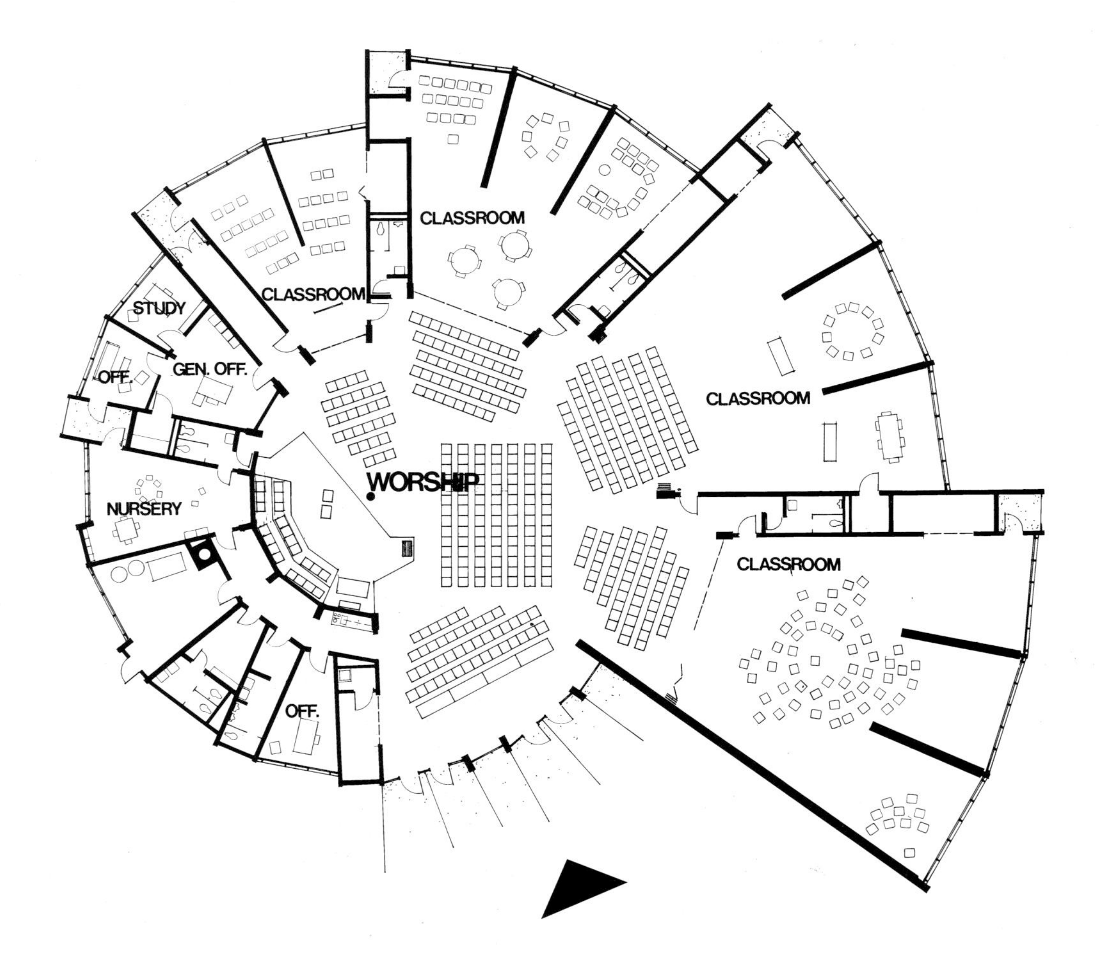

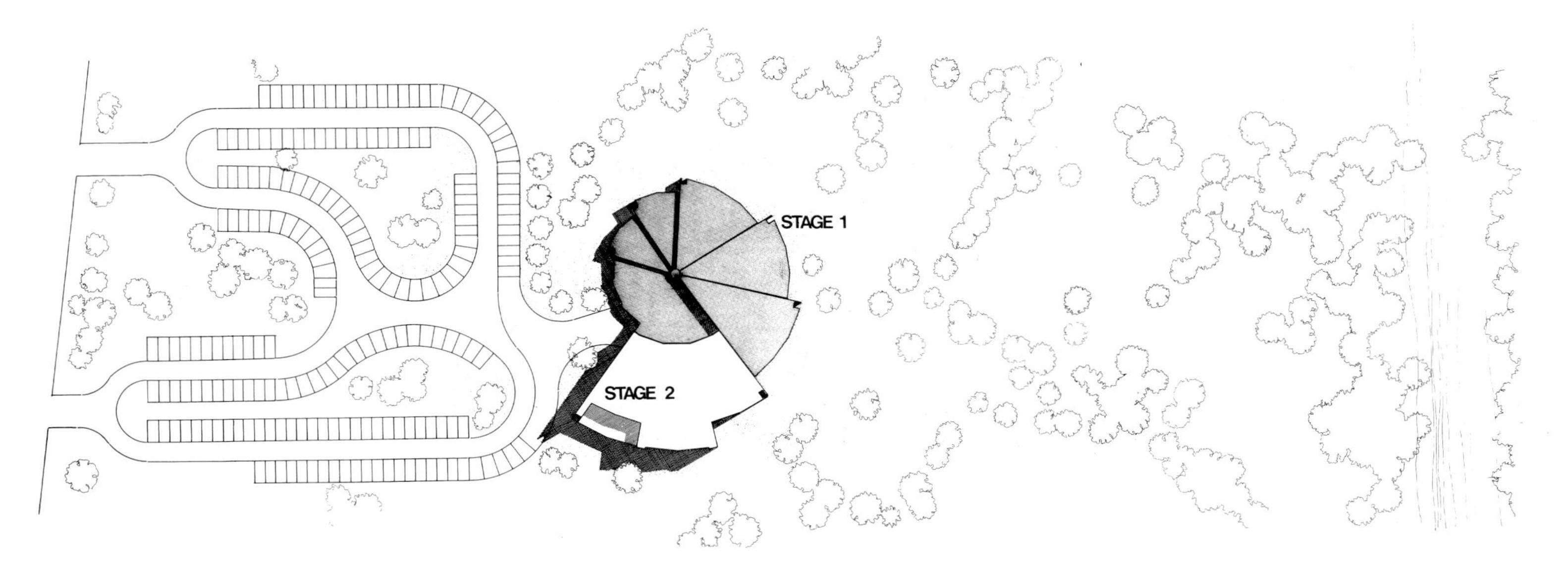

Site plan of the project specifying the various work stages. Left, a detail of the construction showing the careful choice of materials. Opposite page, plan of the building showing the functional distribution of space.

Here and opposite page, two views of inside the church.

A picture of the building showing how it is smoothly inserted in the environment.

KARUNGA MISSION CHURCH
Malawi, Africa
1965

Marianist Missionaries teach at Chaminade Secondary School in Karunga, Malawi, a small south-central African bush community. The problem at hand was to design a Church that embodied all the ideas associated with a renewal of the Liturgy, simultaneously taking into account the climate, scarcity of building materials available and use of native labor.
It was decided to use the simplest geometric configurations and most direct construction methods. A 40' x 40' square ensured an economical exploitation of space, and by placing the Altar directly in the center, 400 people could be seated in only five rows of pews.
The main structure was made out of concrete blocks manufactured by the natives. Masonry piers placed on all four sides acted as the main supports for the wooden trusses, which were also built by local craftsmen out of jungle materials. The metal roof panels were carefully juxtaposed to allow maximum ventilation.

An exterior view of the construction and a project drawing showing a view of the interior space.

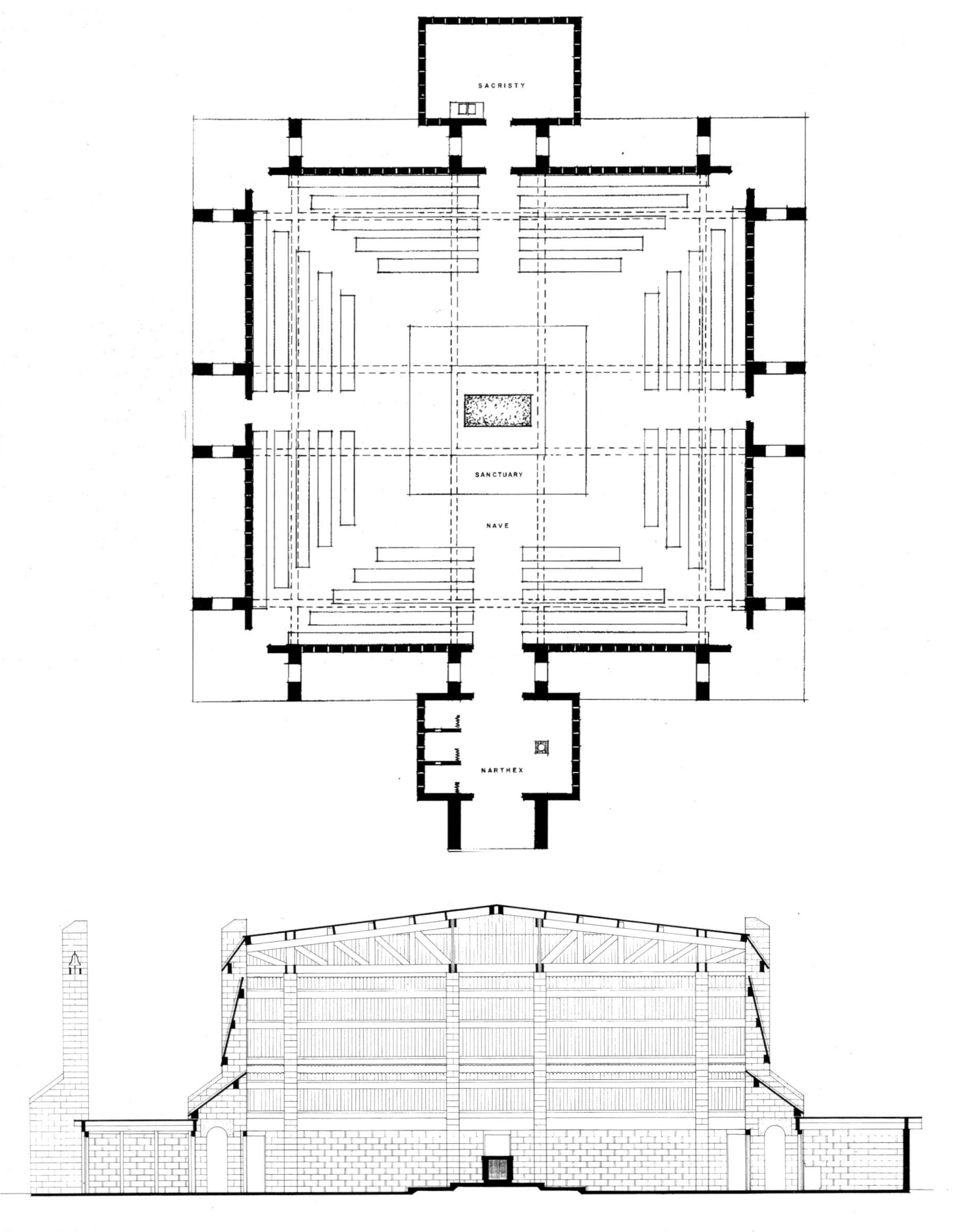

Plan and, below, longitudinal section of the church.

An interior view of the church under construction. The image emphasizes the metal roof panels positioned to filter light and allow proper ventilation.
Below, site plan of the complex.

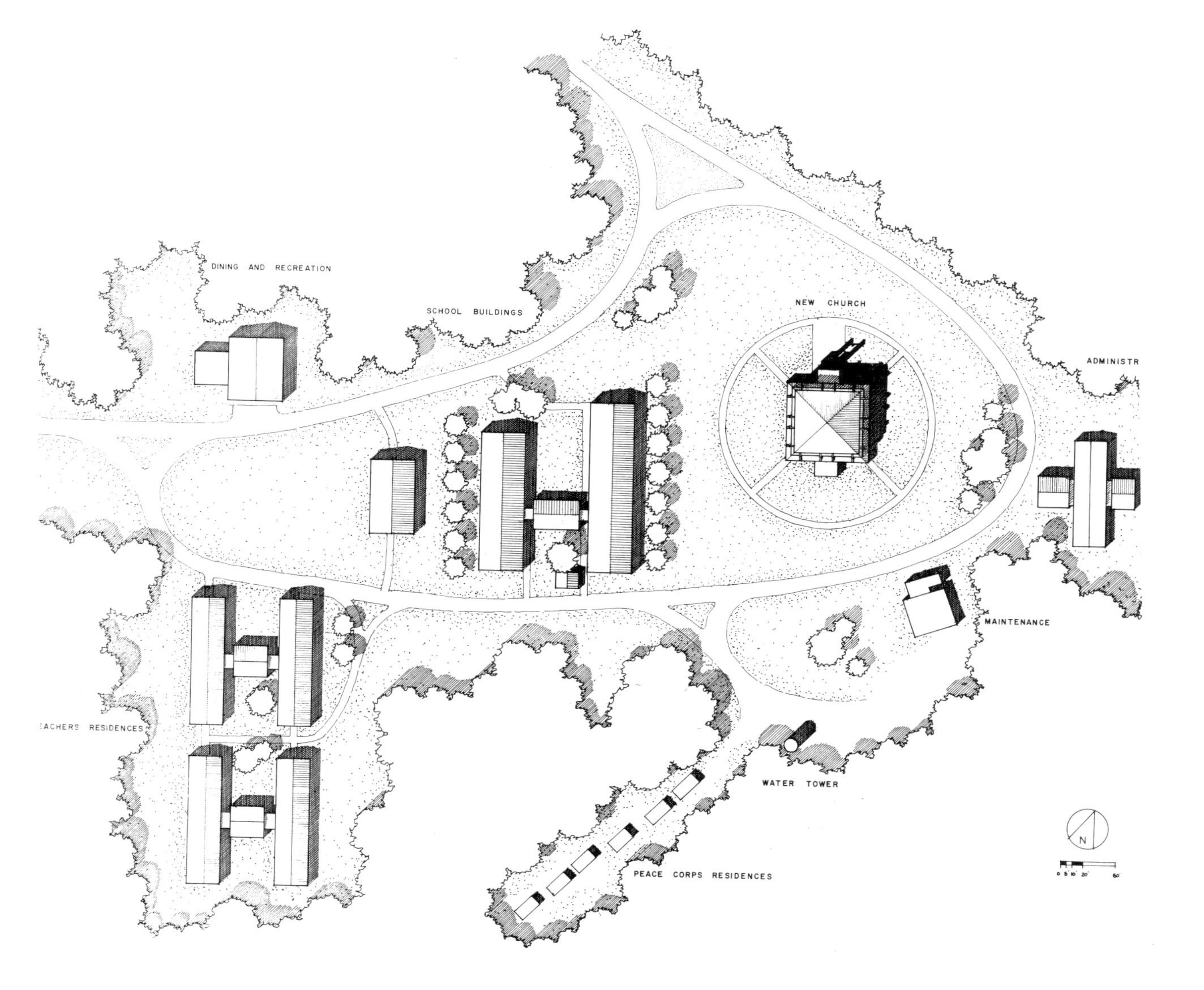

ONTARIO UNITED METHODIST CHURCH
Ontario, Ohio
1966

The initial worship center was built in 1870. The only major addition was constructed in 1954 to accommodate an increase in enrollment for Christian Education. Additional worship space was required reflecting the expanding population in this area of the State. The program stated that the congregation would like to worship in a space that reflects the purpose of the community as they gathered to celebrate and learn Christian doctrine. The shape and silhouette evolved from the diversified program envisioned by the congregation. The selection of chairs, the design of the appointments indicate flexibility that they foresee as a basic requirement for a church of tomorrow.
They proposed the word "Love" which became the theme for the program, a title to express their feelings about the new church building. They also liked to use the word in their art work. For example, individuals sewed patches of personal garmets in artwork such as ties, dresses, blouses, skirts, etc. on a 30' high monks cloth banner located in the chancel of the church. Since love is imperfect the building is a collection of walls that are not parallel. The imperfection is reflected also in the exterior, where the height of walls varies, changing the silhouette of the church building on all sides.

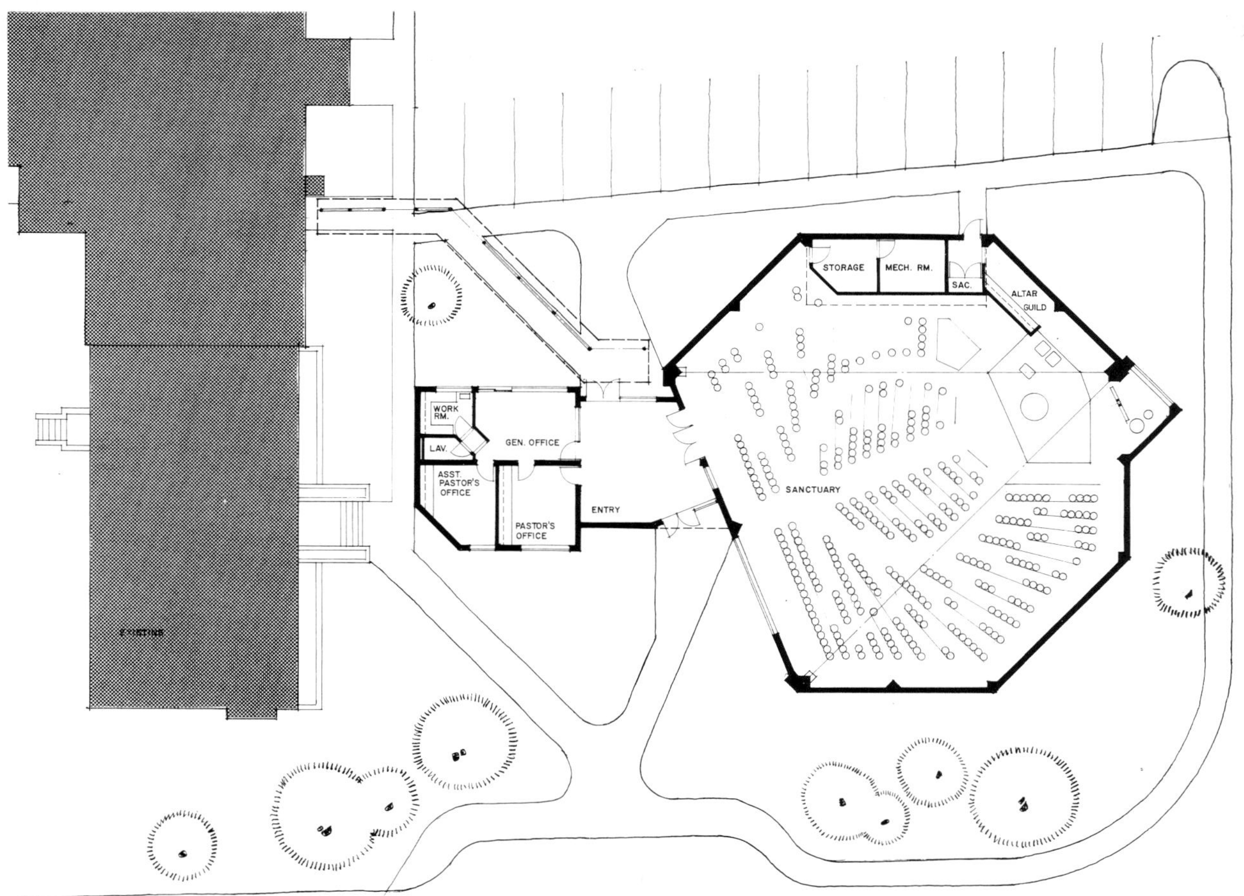

Exterior view of the church showing its non-symmetrical facade. Left, building plan.

Two general view of the interior designed as a flexible open space.

Another view of the building interior emphasizing the intricate ceiling structure.

ST. EDMUND CATHOLIC CHURCH
Warren, Michigan
1966

The program for St. Edmund's was to provide a place of worship with seating room for a Catholic congregation of 1500 people. The Pastor requested that the structure be in character with the community. The population in the immediate environs is approximately 75 per cent Catholic, suggesting that primary importance ought to be placed on the location and silhouette of the Church structure.
In accordance with the guidelines provided in the Constitution of the Sacred Liturgy at the Vatican Council, pride of place was given to the Sanctuary with the congregation gathering around three sides of this area. The location of the Altar for the Sacrifice of the Eucharist and the relative positions of the Repository, Confessionals and Baptistery all hinge around the center of the Church. The simplicity of the square, allowing the roof lines to converge at the center, is an attempt to relate the silhouette of the building to the profiles of the surrounding structures in the local community.
The building's steel frame has a compression ring at the spring line and four huge dormers resting on top. Each dormer represents one of the four gospels.

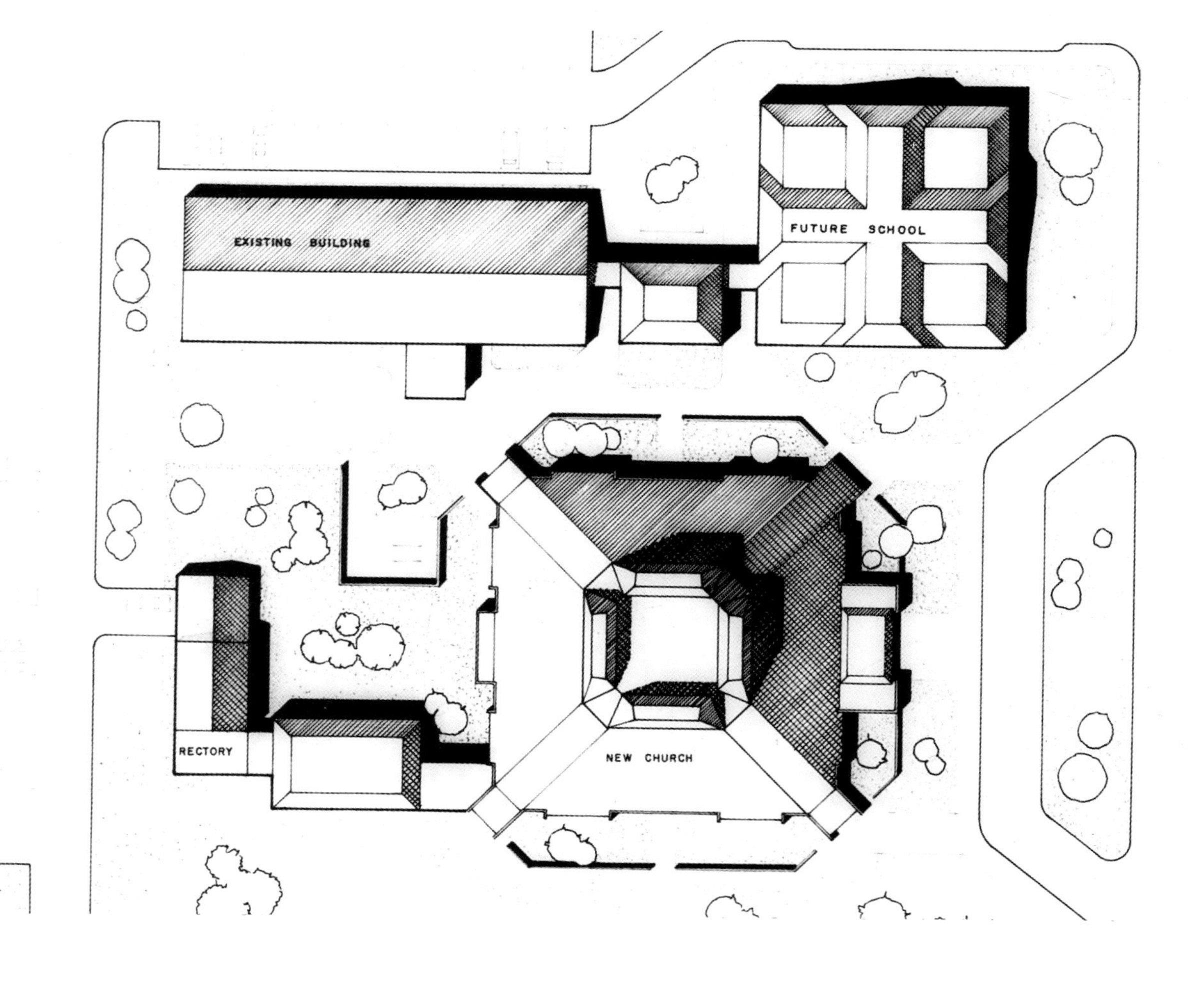

An evocative image of the building immersed in the environment. Opposite page, site plan of the complex.

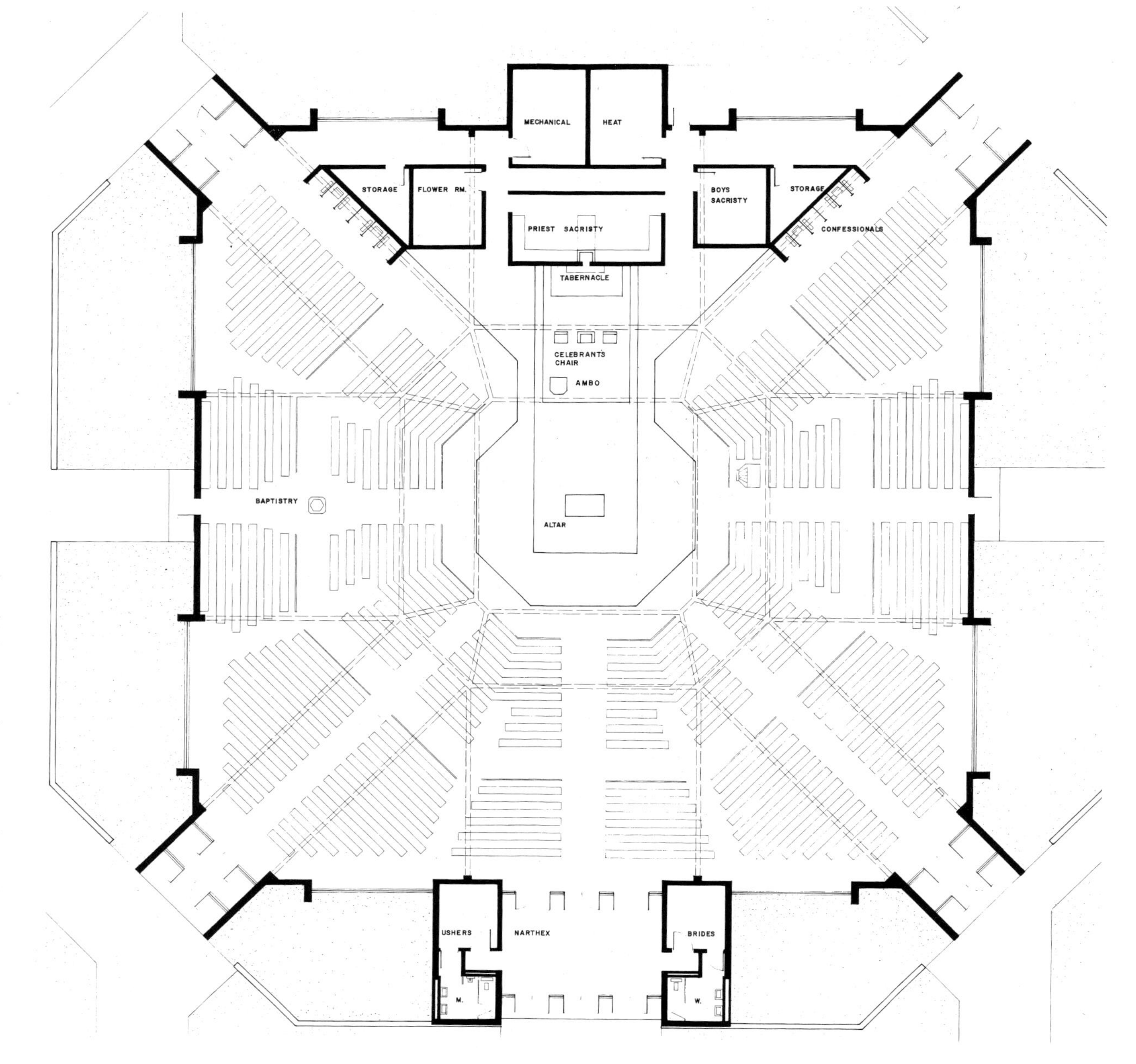

Plan of the church. The building contains 1500 seats.

A view of the altar from the entrance.

KINGSBURY RUN
Cleveland, Ohio
1968

The City of Cleveland, in its desire to plan neighborhoods in blighted areas close to downtown, requested architectural firms to present building strategies that would accommodate housing and retail perceptions which, due to their innovative concepts, would emerge from what was previously referred to as "pioneering areas."
RFA proposed a resident development in areas that needed immediate attention.
The result was a monolith structure combining housing, retail and office space in order to create a new neighborhood of approximately 2,500 in proximity to downtown Cleveland.

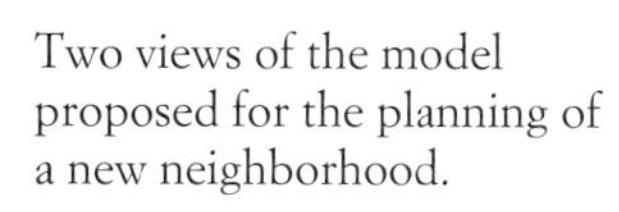

Two views of the model proposed for the planning of a new neighborhood.

PIONEER MEMORIAL CHURCH
Solon, Ohio
1969

The juxtaposition of the building and the relationship between the various structural elements ensure the kind of flexibility required for a varied program. The driveway and parking areas are positioned to complement the existing topography and blend in with the overall plan concept devised by the community of Solon.
The structure is also designed to accommodate a logical and unlimited expansion program reflecting the continued growth in this community.
The basic units of the program are visually accessible at all times under one single roof. All the most significant areas are open and free flowing, as stipulated in the rigorous design plan. The Sanctuary is defined by a glass wall at the Narthex. There is total interaction between every member of the congregation in all the various spaces, creating a sense of united purpose within a community of worship.

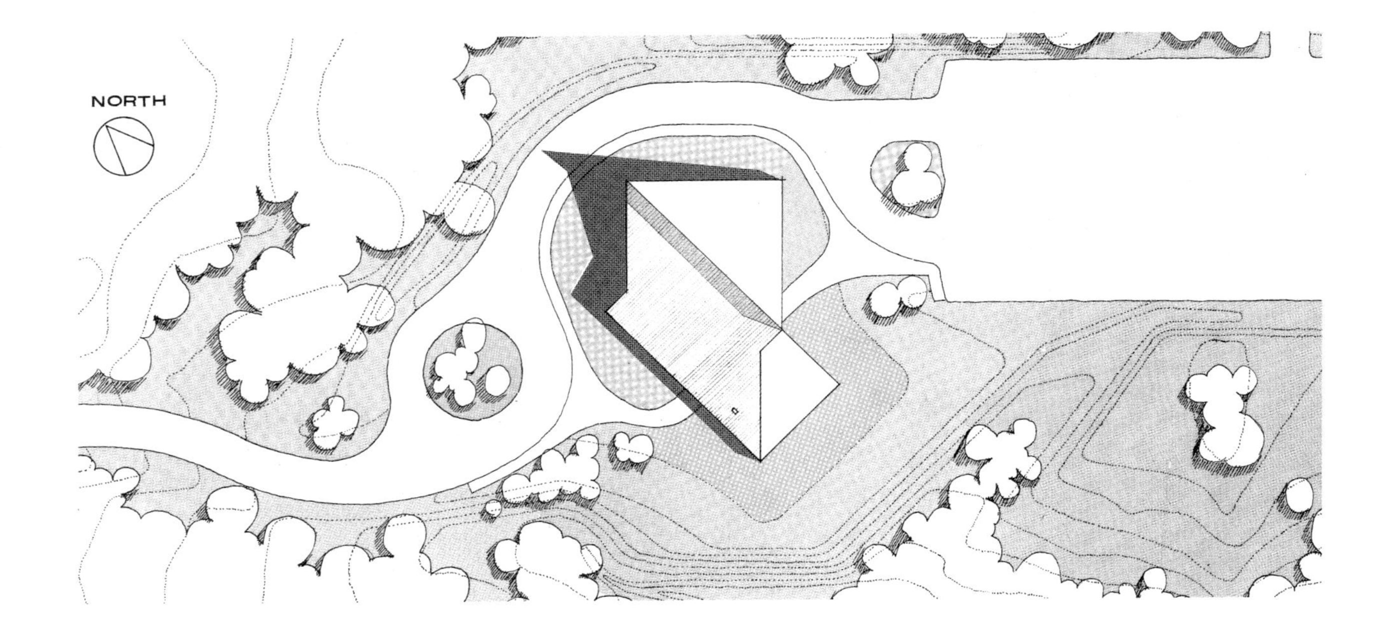

Main facade of the building seen from the street. Opposite page, site plan of the construction.

The entrance of the church from the parking lot. Bottom of page, plan showing the arrangement of functional areas.

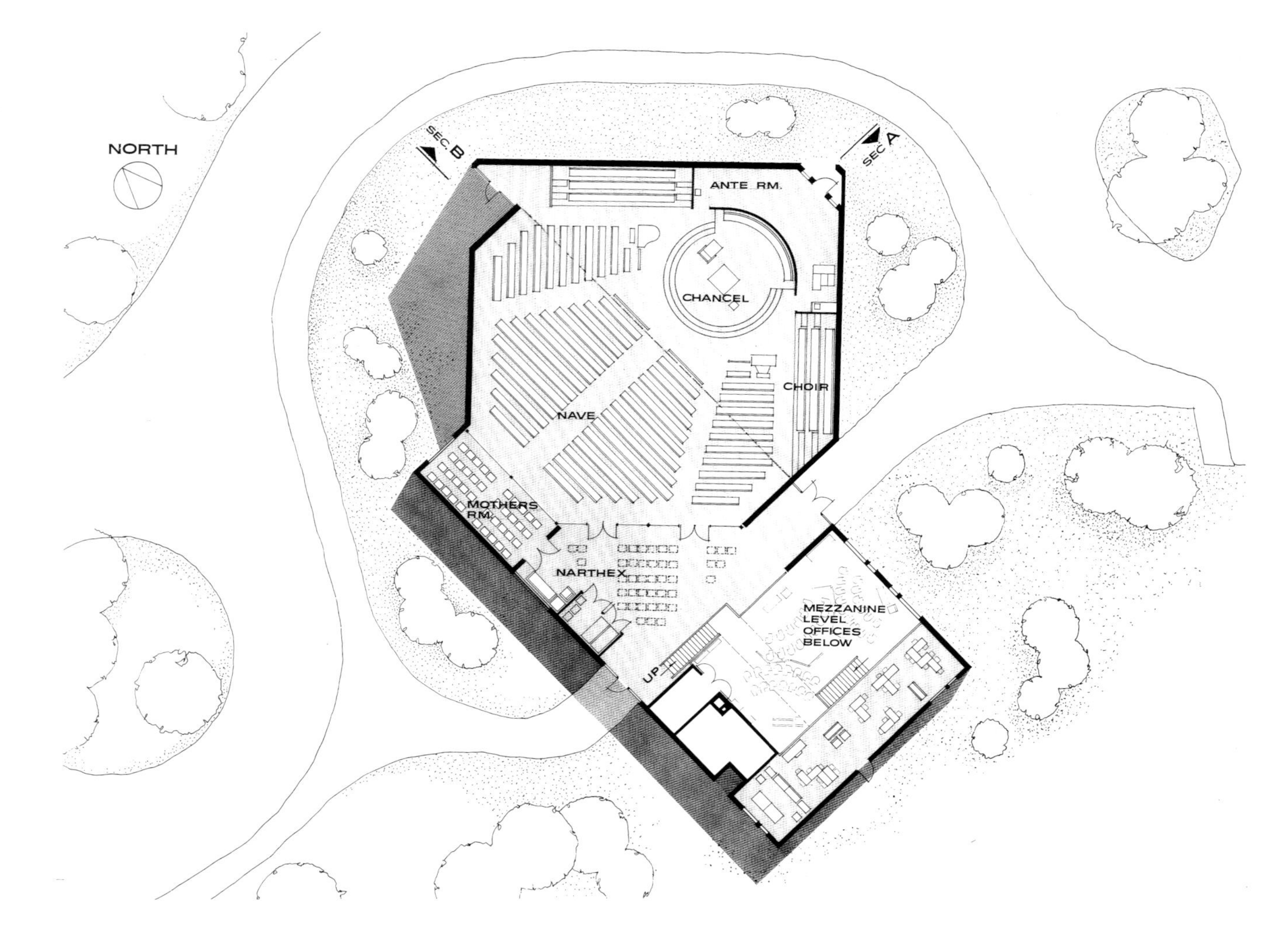

A picture of the nave with the chancel.

VILLA ANGELA ACADEMY
Cleveland, Ohio
1969

Villa Angela Academy can accommodate an enrollment of 1,000 girls and replaces the 94-year-old Academy located on a 55-acre wooded site in an urban area. The building's main open space is composed of interrelated areas representing stages in the learning process laid down by the Ursuline Sisters and the Educational Research Council.
They can be defined as follows: (1) a research area containing printed material, audio-visual information and teacher consultation facilities; (2) a laboratory and instruction areas, including Large Group Instruction for 800; and (3) individual study areas containing carrels, personal storage facilities, seating and tables.
The idea was to create a positive learning center, rather than anonymous classrooms. The individual study and laboratory/group instruction areas surround the research area on three sides. All areas are located on different levels and flow into each other in an open arrangement. The only closed areas are the Music Room, Auditorium, and other ancillary spaces housing department centers, storage facilities, etc. The gymnasium is only separated from the education facilities by a change in level and movable bleachers.
A twenty-five foot structural grid reflects the "pod" dimensions proposed by the educators. The only exception to the column grid is in the Auditorium and Gymnasium. The Auditorium contains a large thrust stage and can be divided into three Lecture Rooms. The backstage area connects the scenery shops, make-up room, storage space and dressing rooms to the shower rooms and other storage areas for physical education, allowing multiple use of the facilities. In all, the structure houses six open levels providing a variety of spaces to encourage student interaction.
In 1990 the Ursuline Sisters community sold the property to the Cleveland Public Library. They transformed the building into two multi-use library facilities.

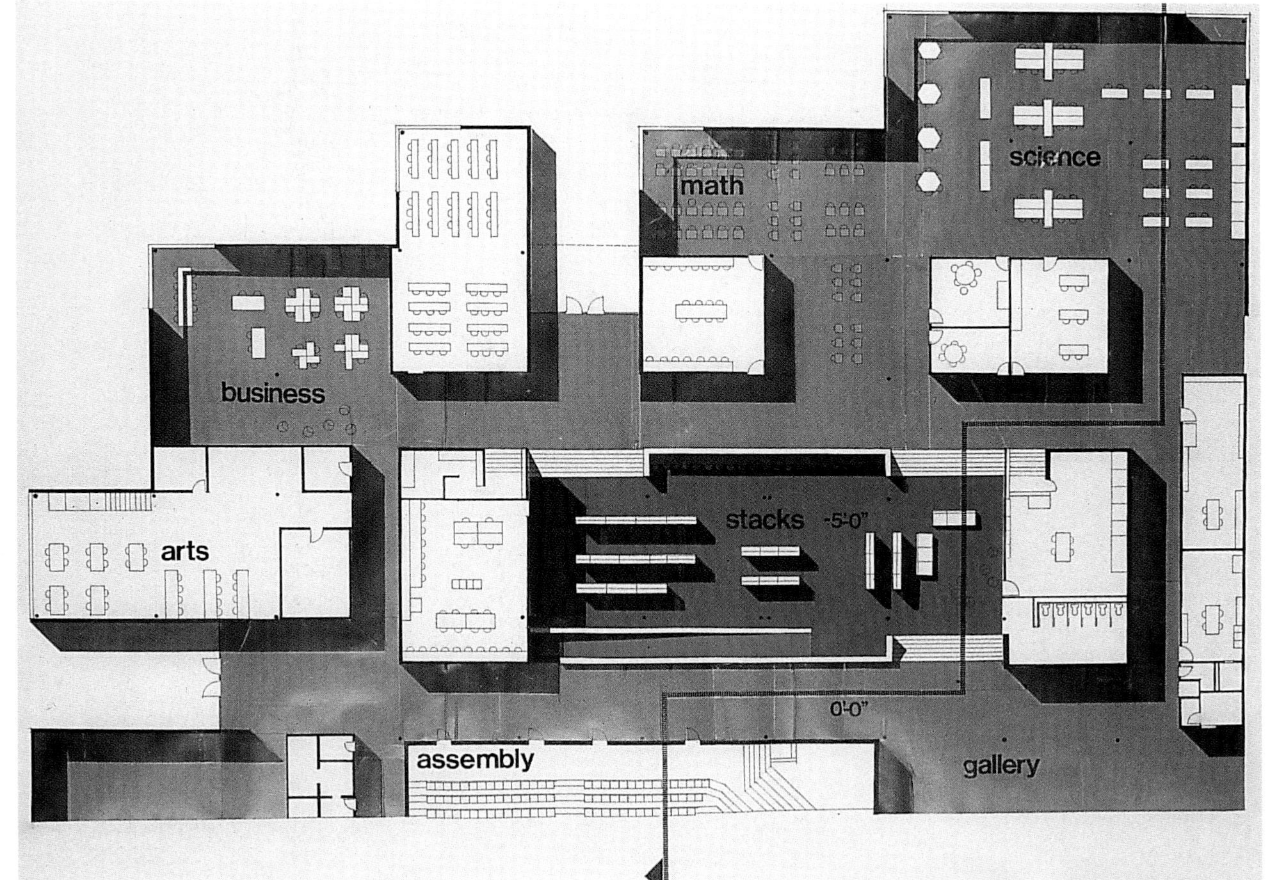

Above, an exterior view of the building. Left, volumetric plan of the main level. Opposite page, a sketch showing a perspective view of the complex.

Three pictures of the wide interior functional spaces.

CHURCH OF THE COVENANT AND HALLINAN CENTER
Cleveland, Ohio
1969

The Church of the Covenant addition and its plaza were integrated with an existing design for a sunken plaza to be built by the University Circle Foundation, a parking garage, and the Newman Center adjacent to the Case Western Reserve University campus. The design was stimulated by the abandonment of property lines and the incorporation of a major pedestrian artery linking the north and south campuses.

The program was to provide additional educational space for a 1909 parish hall designed by Ralph Cramm. Recognizing the quality of the Gothic design, the challenge was to create a comparable new addition which would provide classrooms to sustain an expanding religious program.

The Hallinan Center was the final addition to the plaza complex. The problem was not just to ensure the Hallinan Center enhanced the plaza and complemented the geometrical layout of the existing buildings, but also to respect the pedestrian paths meandering through this urban space. The challenge was further complicated by the fact the plaza and three buildings defining it each had a different owner.

The program for the Hallinan Center required the construction of two flexible areas, one for worship and recreational activities and the other to serve as a lounge and counseling area. The Hallinan Center was designed with sufficient transparency to make the plaza and recreational-worship area one continuous space, with the lounge area suspended over this space in the form of a mezzanine. This creates a variety of visual spaces inviting pedestrian involvement. The building responds to the need for young people to express their commitment to the community.

A partial view of the new construction showing the adjacent buildings. Opposite page, section of the project incorporated in its architectural context.

Bottom of page, plan at plaza level and, above, plan at upper level.

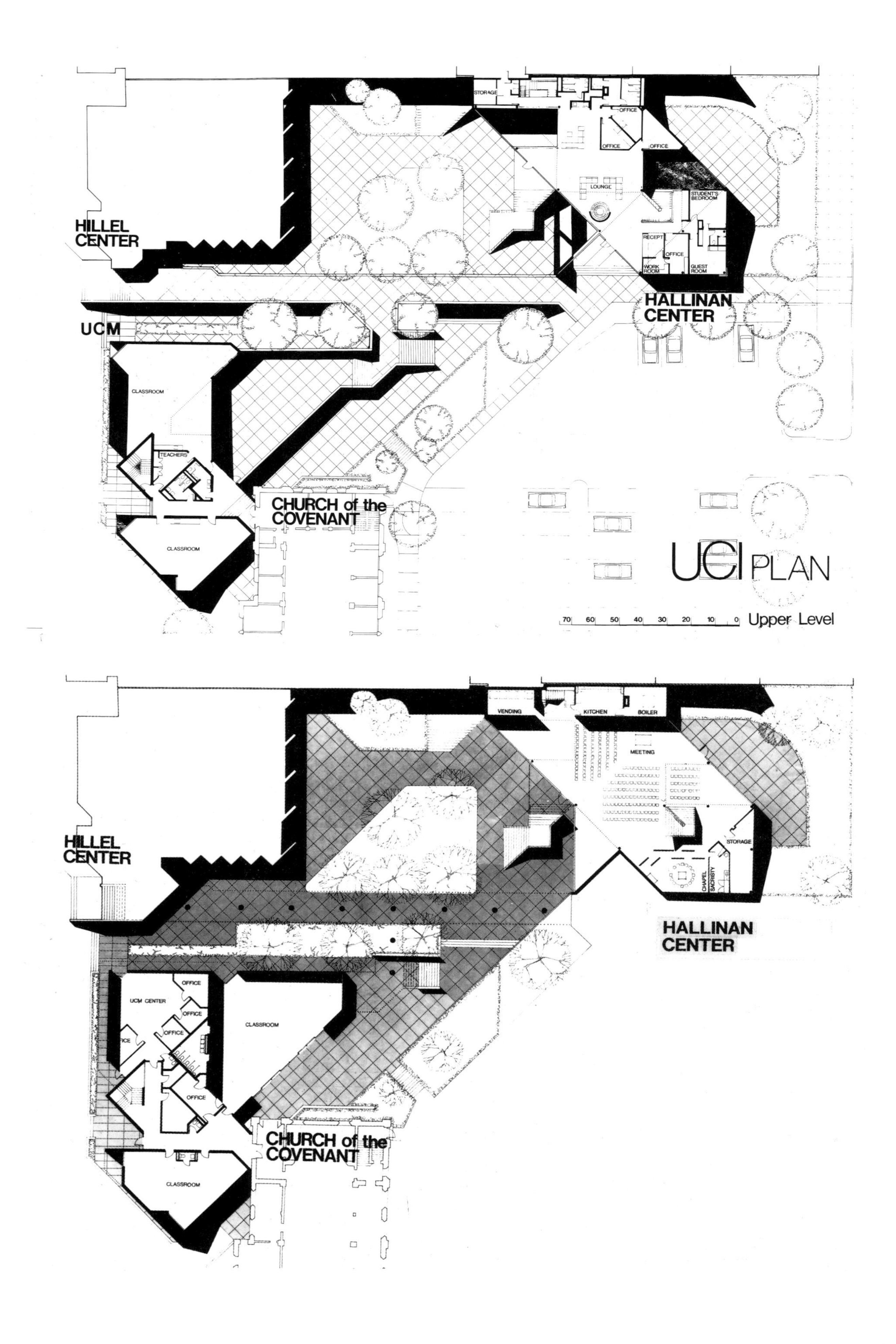

Two pictures of the building showing the entrance steps to the church addition.

ST. ELIZABETH'S CATHOLIC CHURCH
Columbus, Ohio
1971

A conventional parish structure could not meet the specific needs of this congregation, as outlined by the Building Council. The spatial layout of St. Elizabeth's evolved from a thorough analysis of the program drawn up to embody the community's desire to express its Christian commitment. A large pavilion provides flexible space around a fixed core. The pavilion is used for worship, education, Christian fellowship, meetings, and meditation.
As the capacity of these functions varies, so will the area required to accommodate them. The intrinsic flexibility of the design is reinforced by a library/lounge where individuals can meet for study times and other small-group activities. It also provides an area where the community can assemble together before worship.
The vertical core contains a chapel for the preservation of the Blessed Sacrament. It also serves as a place where small numbers of people can meet to celebrate mass.

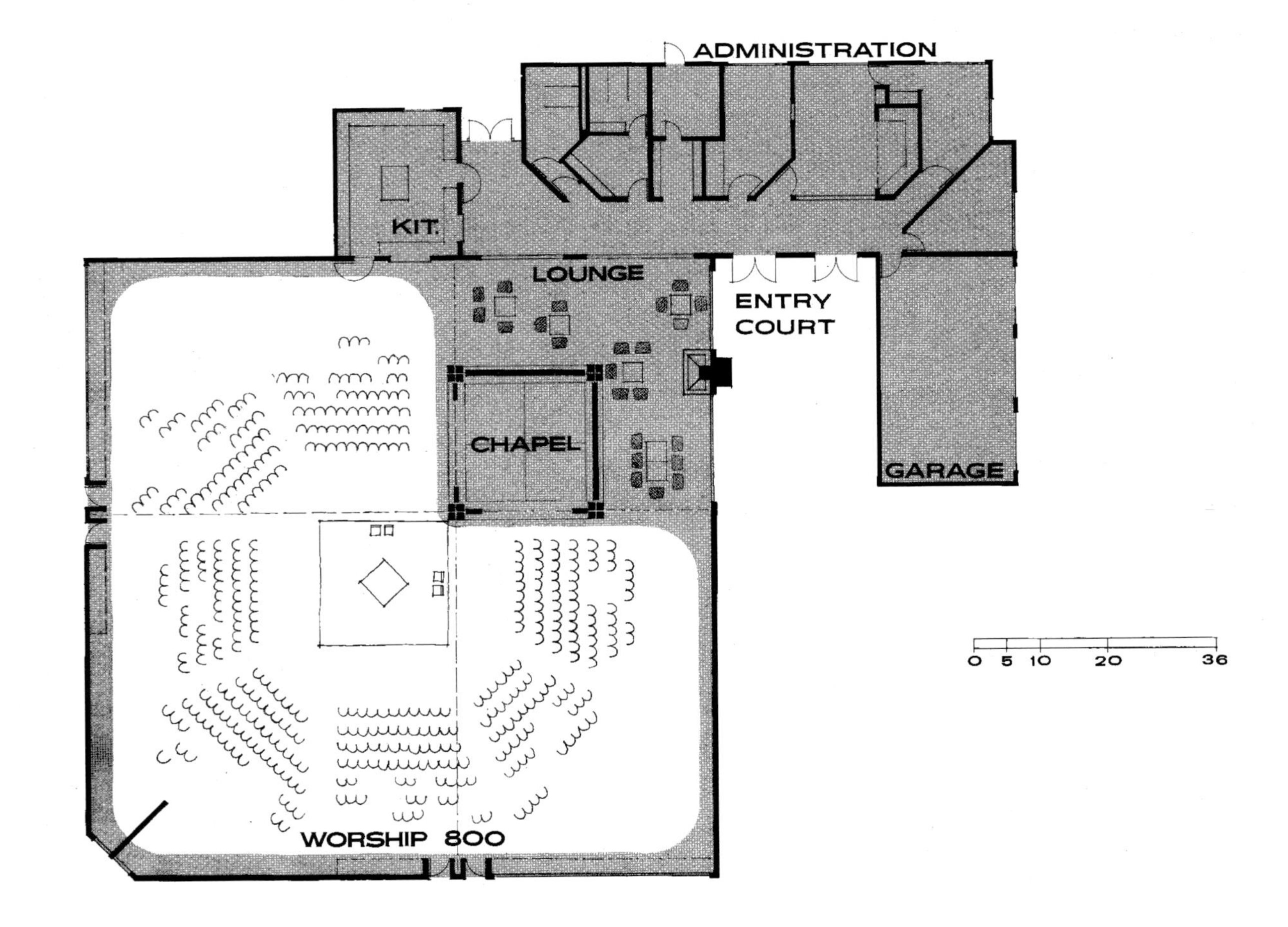

The building seen from the outside. Below, three project designs with different spatial solutions. Opposite page, ground floor plan.

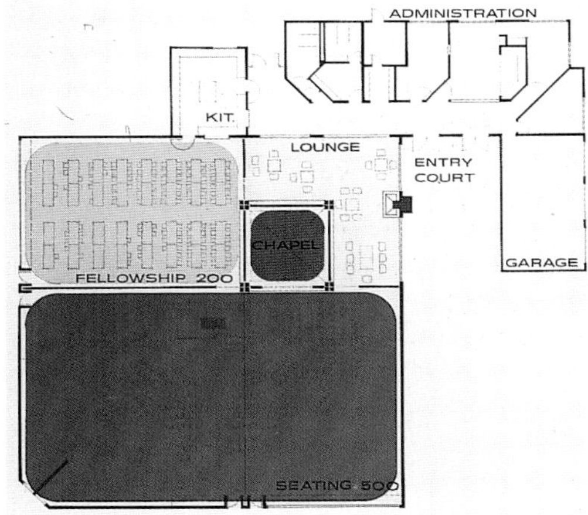

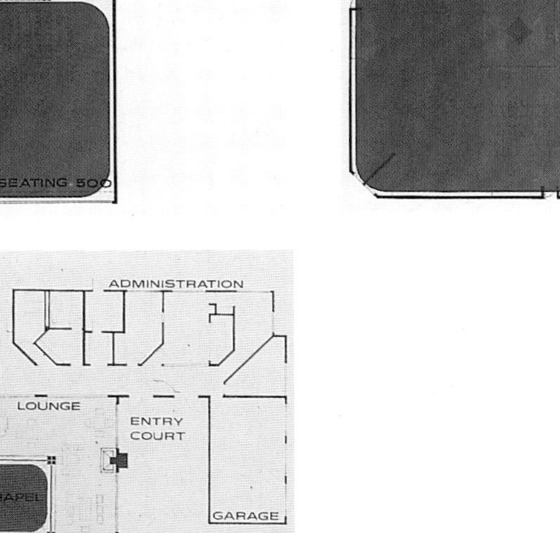

Two pictures of the flexible, multifunctional interior space.

ST. PASCHAL BAYLON CHURCH
Highland Heights, Ohio
1971 - 1996

The Church incorporates a space concept that allows people to share. A sixty-foot-high glass wall forms a major segment of the geometric shape of the building. This transparent, yet reflective wall permits the community to be aware of the function of the building. It also makes them realize the value of community worship. People are reflected in the exterior mirrored wall. This reflection expresses the vitality of the Church in our community.
The worship center is shaped like a Greek theatre with the participants arranged around the 1200-seat Sanctuary. The Sacraments are located in areas contiguous with the glass wall. Their position in the interior space reflects the liturgical life of the community. The Altar of Sacrifice is centrally located. The location of the Ambo permits visual access to the entire congregation and is near the Celebrant's Choir. We must remember the Church is a teaching center. The word and its place of presentation are symbolically represented in the building design. The Sacrament of Baptism and Penance are also expressed in the silhouette of the wall. The Chapel is a separate space holding the Blessed Sacrament that also provides overflow seating when required.
The Church is located between the existing Seminary and school buildings providing a conduit for unity as well as the focal point of the entire religious complex.
The Church is a steel frame structure with a wooden deck and Ludowici tile roof. The mirrored walls are constructed of light and heat reflecting glass. The pedestrian plaza around the new facility will act as a transition area between the parking facility and new building. The 70-foot-high structure culminates in the glass clerestory which permits light to illuminate the interior regardless of the time of day. Artificial lighting will complement this concept of natural light. Currently the parish plans to build a side chapel for everyday services.

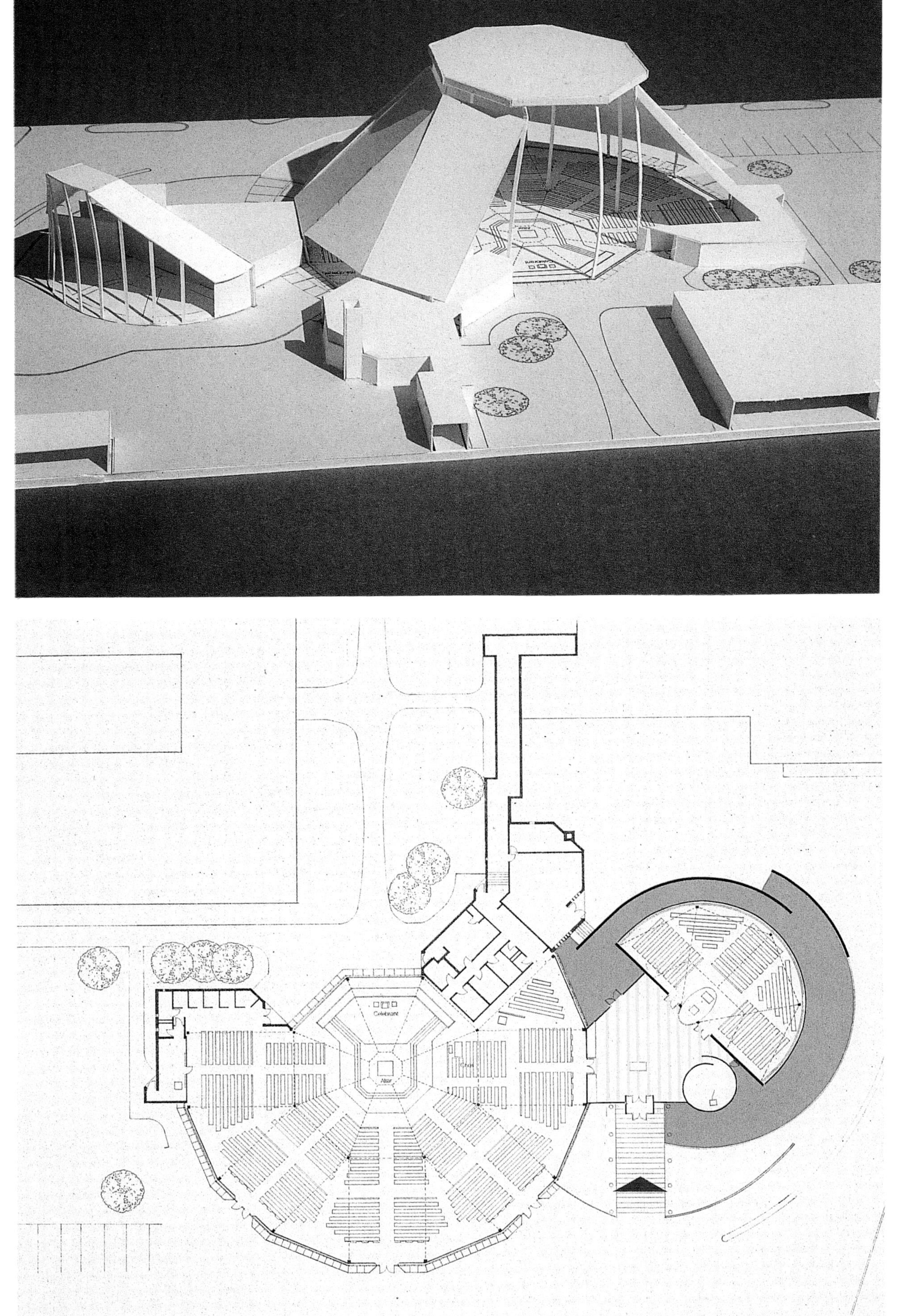

Top of page, a model of the entire complex showing the planned extension, a new project by Fleischman. Bottom of page, building plan showing the extension.

Two external views of the main church, with the glass facade acting as a transparent as well as reflecting filter.

Two images of the interior space overflown by natural light thanks to the ample glass facade.

BELLFLOWER ELEMENTARY SCHOOL
Mentor, Ohio
1973

Mark Twain said: "Too bad a young man's education has to be interrupted to go to school." The Superintendent wished to reflect this thought by providing an educational center that incorporated many of the ideas found in small villages. He believed in open planning, but did not want an anonymous space for learning.

He wanted to create openness to provide ungraded class areas, using the team teaching concept - one master working with three other teachers and volunteers for groups of 100 students.

The building was constructed on a flat 54-acre site completely surrounded by one-story structures. A characteristic of the community is the band of single-story masonry structures creating a relentlessly monotonous pattern throughout. The chosen solution contradicts the apparent rigidity through the construction of an earth building or non-building. The structure is approximately 200 x 200 feet with the exterior wall constructed in the form of an earth beam. The modules measure 40 x 40 feet. The roof is built out of a light-weight steel beam and bar joist framework covered with Tectum. The vertical material inserted between the top of the berm and underside of the steel is made of insulated metal panels and a continuous band of glass. This system of building provided an economical enclosure and allowed the School Board and Administration to consider adding on an additional 15,000 square feet for the cost of building a traditional school.

Since the program brief specified the need for an open school with a variety of educational spaces delineated by numerous learning alcoves, the concept of an Educational City seemed to be the logical direction to take. The main axis of the plan created two large avenues called Market and Main Streets, brought to life by trees, lamp posts and traffic lights.

A learning center has been located at each corner of the City, and a tiered theatre constructed at the periphery from the concrete carpet following the pitch of the berm.

The mezzanine connected by an open staircase provides four distinct spaces each overlooking the learning laboratories.

The captain's deck and administration/work area stand at the very center of the site. The focal point allows visual access to all areas.

The playground is located inside, with a 40-foot square skylight at the entrance, providing a natural area equipped with planting and recreational facilities. Here students can enjoy a short break in the picturesque park setting or attend informal classes.

The net result is a learning center bringing the city into the classroom through mounds of earth. The entrances are tunnels bored through the earth berm and the building is symmetrically-shaped to reflect a systems approach to construction. Inside, an indefinite number of spaces provide staff with several options for a total learning process - and a multitude of spatial and educational experiences for children to enjoy. The building not only evokes positive reactions from both students and teachers, it has also been enthusiastically received by non-school groups as well.

From top of page down, plan of the mezzanine, plan of the ground floor and cross section of the building. Following page, an exterior detail showing the entrance.

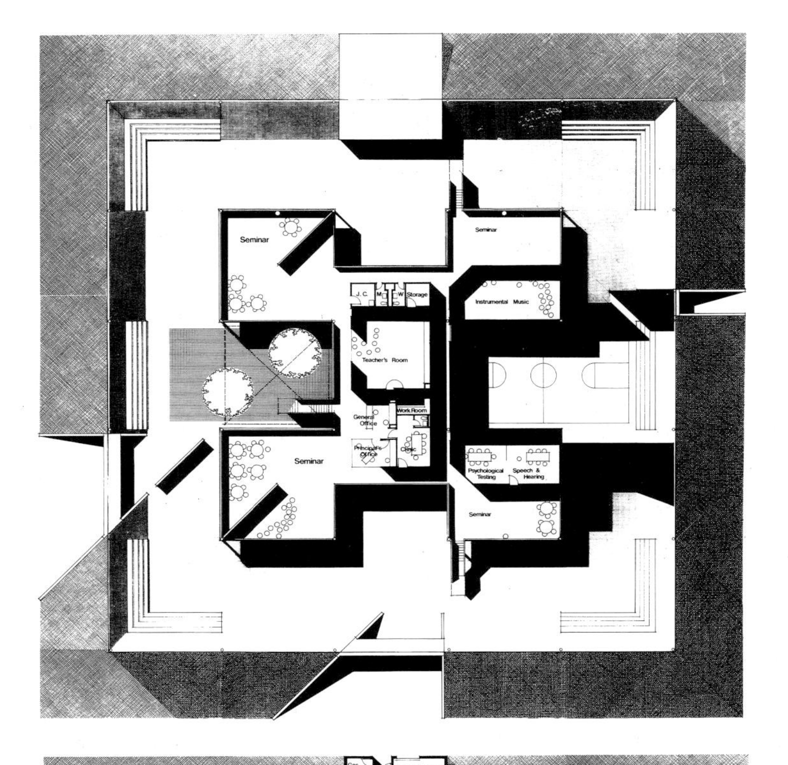

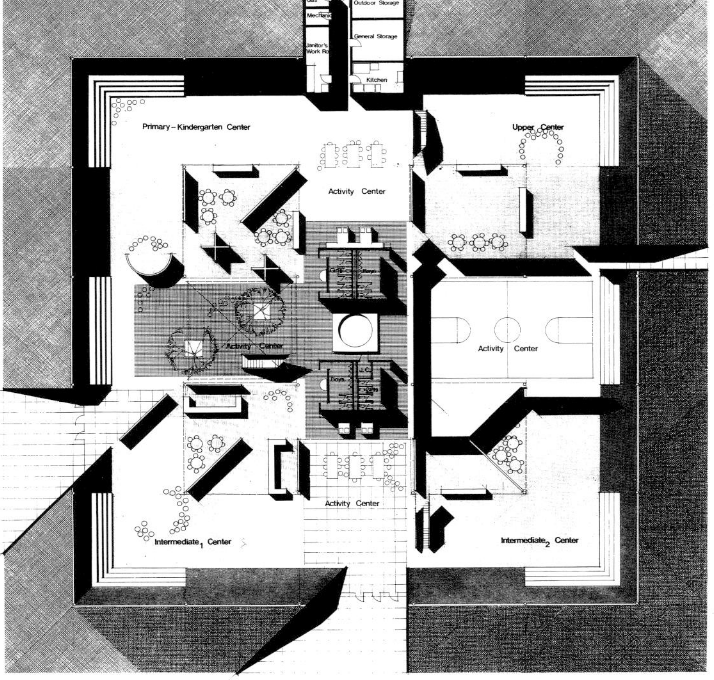

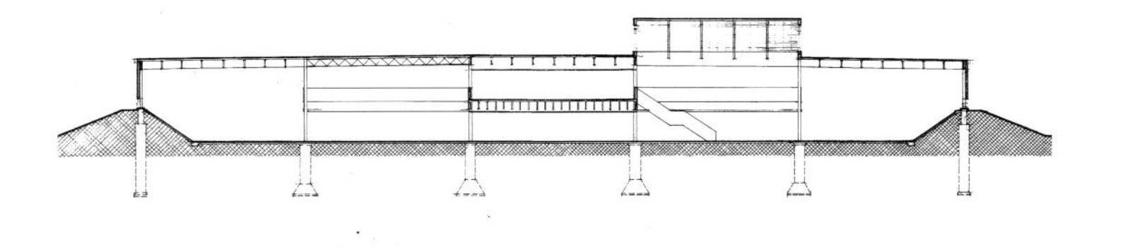

Entrance of the building. Opposite page, another view of the interior showing the work and play areas.

CHRIST THE KING LUTHERAN CHURCH
North Olmsted, Ohio
1973

The congregation wanted to provide a place of worship where people could share together. The building committee initially concentrated on commissioning the construction of a new sanctuary where the entire congregation would be able to meet together in ceremonial worship. The new 500-seat sanctuary allows every member of the congregation to gather in close proximity to the central altar.
The original project was designed around a triangular geometric form, which seemed to best reflect the goals of this church.
The colored glass used in the skylight is designed to mirror the liturgical symbols of the contemporary church. The symbolism is further emphasized by faceted color. The glass helps diffuse light throughout the building structures, creating a unified whole designed once again to embody the goals of this congregational family.
The sanctuary has been designed to create the illusion of not being supported by the church building. The decision to position this space in a directly accessible "loft area" seems to symbolically express the uncomplicated objectives of the church members.
It was decided to locate the educational area in the basement. The walls surrounding these educational spaces actually support the floor of the nave.
Not only does the sanctuary provide an ideal place for celebrating religion, it also constantly reminds the congregation of its underlying purpose as a community for worship, fellowship and education. Families immediately identify their church as being the center of their activities. The spatial credibility resulting from the clever juxtaposition of the sanctuary walls and glass, in unison with the subordinate structure as a whole, attests to the congregation's desire to create a living structure for sharing in the pure and simple pageantry of worship.

Exterior view of the church showing an incisive image of the symbolic cross.

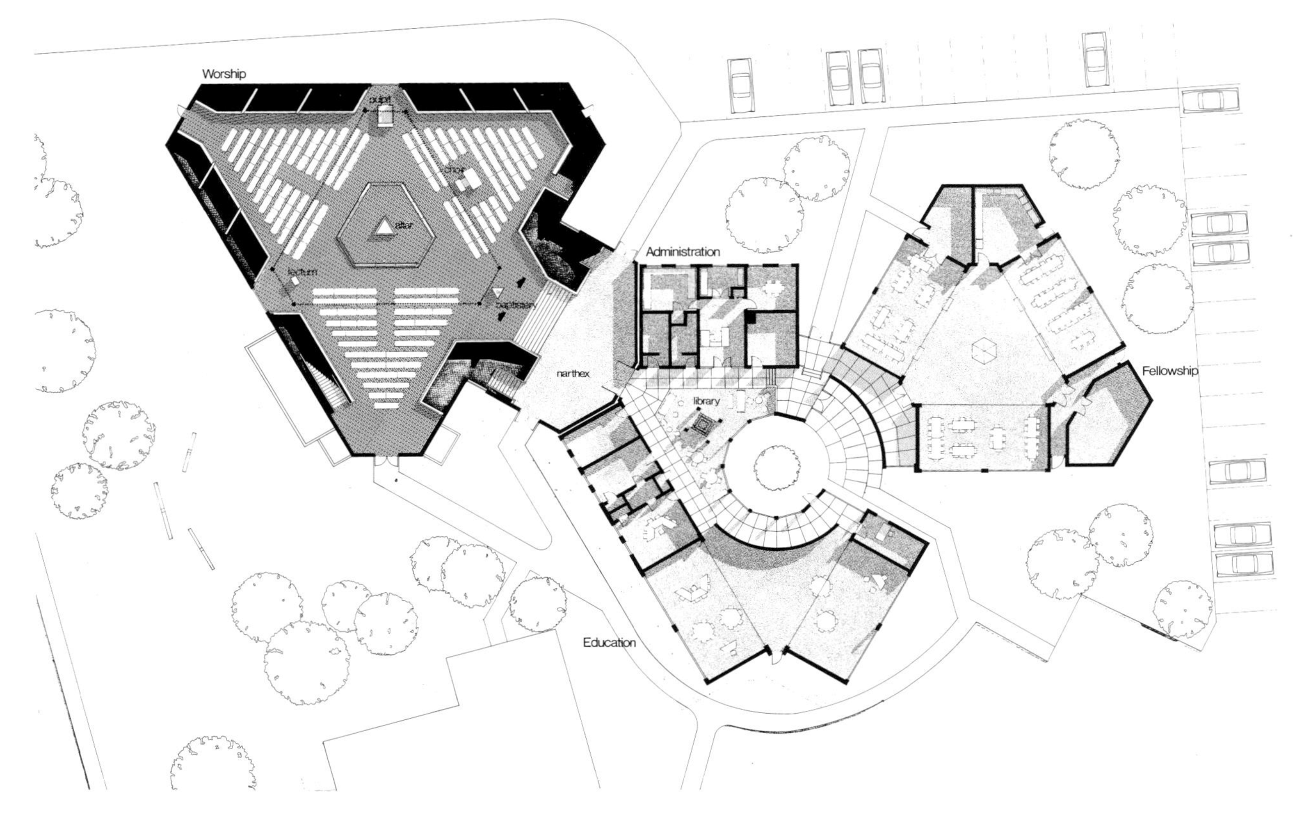

Site plan of the complex. Following pages, the interior of the church showing details of the glass windows.

KENT STATE UNIVERSITY
MEMORIAL GYMNASIUM ANNEX
Kent, Ohio
1974

The facility at Kent State University recognizes the philosophy that physical education generates energy - the open laboratory challenges participants to learn by doing and by seeing. Within the building unfolds fluid views of energetic motion with each turn of a corner, walk up a ramp or pause on a platform. The spaces encourage participation through strategic placement of activities which seem casually located but which, upon closer inspection, reveal purposeful and sympathetic treatment.
The concept of integrated openness permits all of the various activities to be organized in general proximity to the new and existing locker rooms, and to be viewed from one space to another. Included in the complex are teaching gymnasiums, instructional swimming pool, hardball courts, combatives room, dance studios, classrooms, laboratories, faculty offices, and administrative areas.

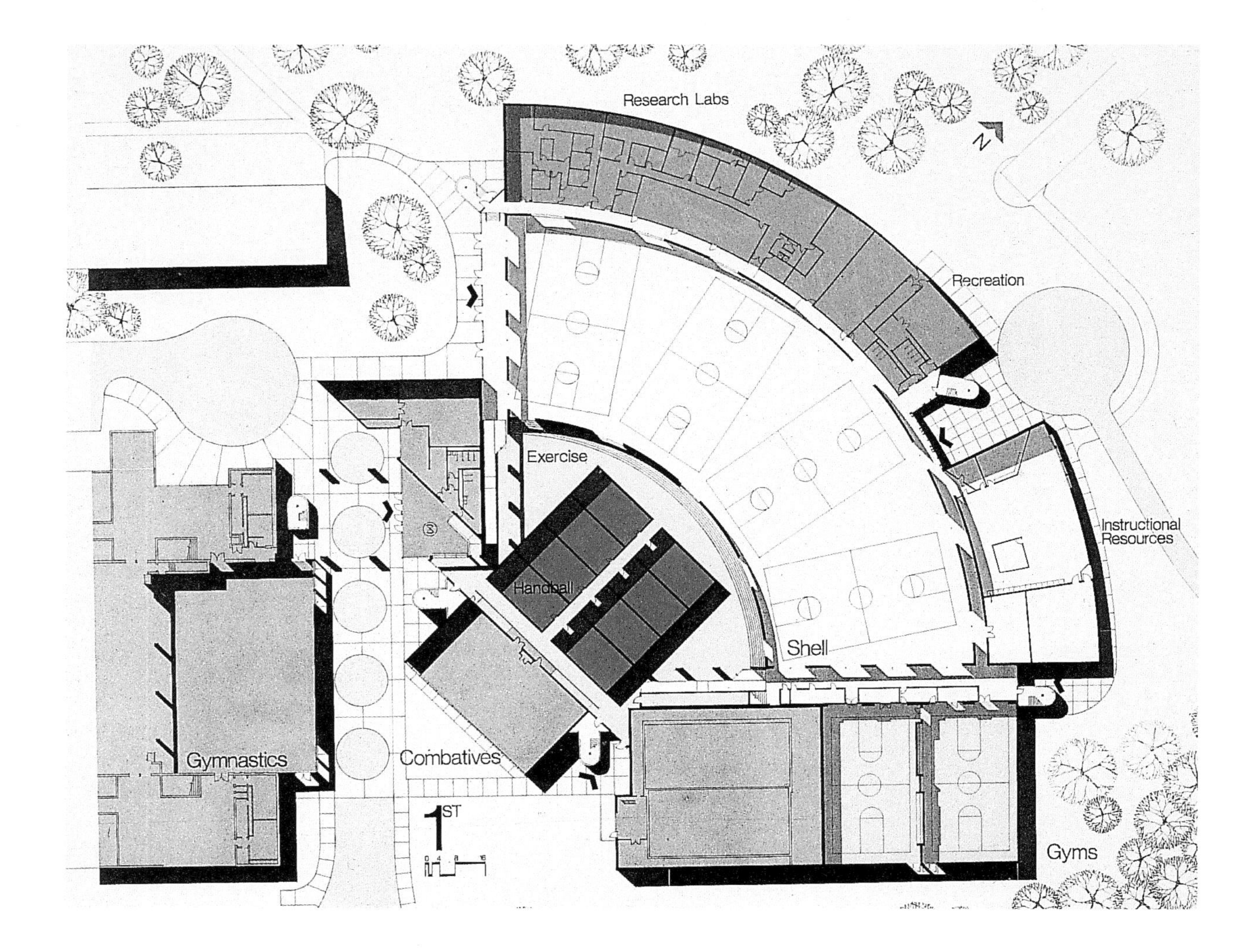

Exterior view of the building with the glass windows which open onto the indoor playgrounds. Opposite page, plan of the complex.

Exterior view of the gymnastic facilitiy.

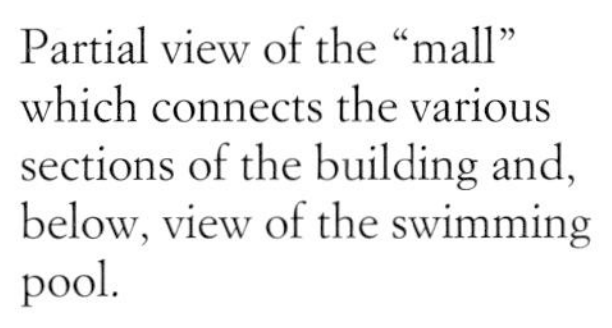

Partial view of the "mall" which connects the various sections of the building and, below, view of the swimming pool.

ADP
Independence, Ohio
1979

A national data processing organization required a midwest regional office facility to perform computer services for various industrial, education and health care clients. Located on a sloped site in a tree-covered area housing zones for business services, the machine-like design reflects the efficient computer process conducted within. The 24-hour data processing operation requires a secure, shirt-sleeve environment, one that encourages constant communication among management, data staff and computer professionals. Multi-levels permit various operational activities to be visually evident.

Although the structure's appearance represents machine-age technology, design efficiency does not rule out human concerns. The physical and mental fatigue normally associated with data processing tasks requires spaces providing relief from occupational stress. The floating lunch cafe, located in the center of the activities, affords employees the opportunity of taking essential breaks in order to enhance their performance. This public area acts as a horizontal and vertical access for the handicapped, as well as a strong, unifying design element.

The varying topography and abundance of birch, scotch pine, white pine and maple trees provide an interesting contrast for this structural machine. The parking area is integrated into the hillside and permits immediate access into the facility at the lowest level. Transparent areas are oriented to the east and south side of the building, taking advantage of the panoramic view and solar energy available. In deference to the prevailing wind from the northwest, solid walls are provided at this section.

Ten years later a major addition was completed to complement the initial phase of construction. The various functions were easily expanded and the exterior material was black-coloured in contrast to the aluminum appearance of the structure.

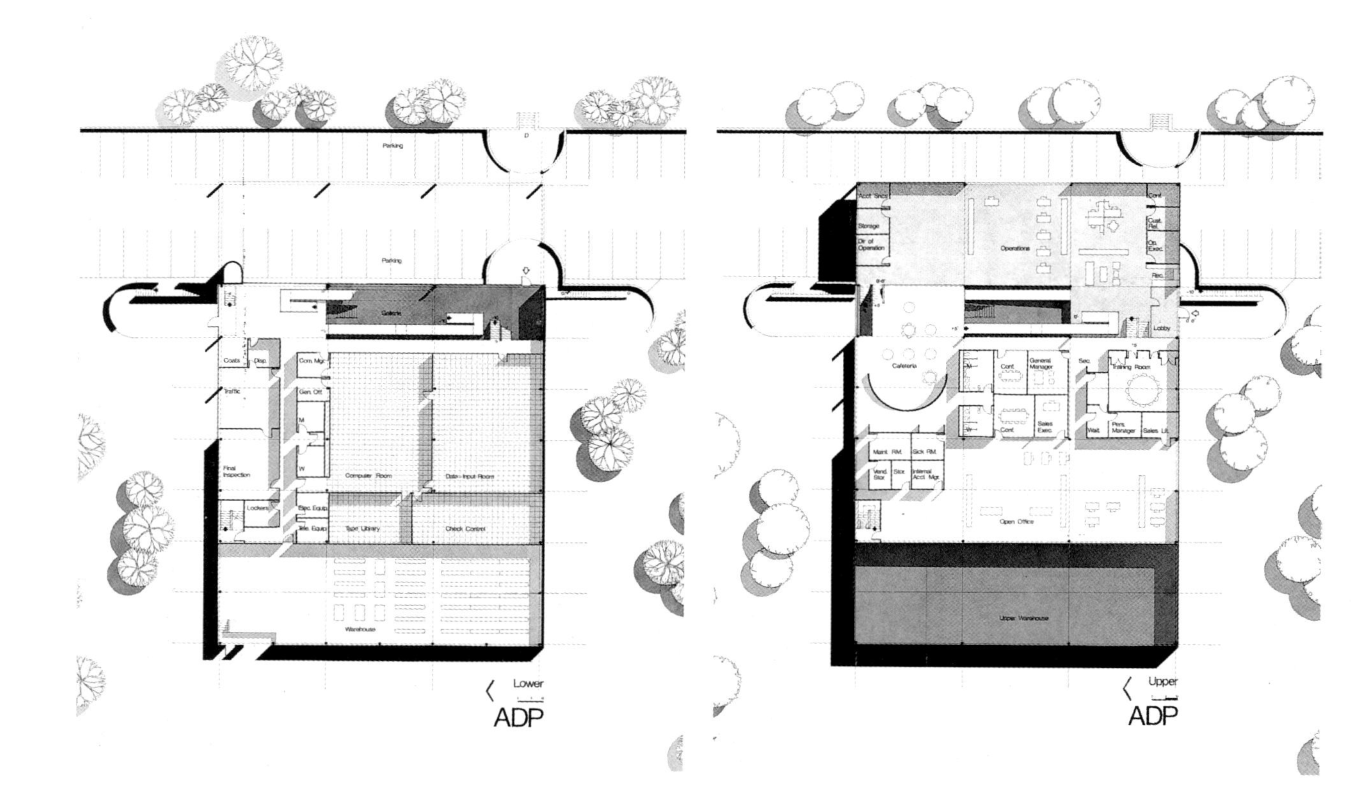

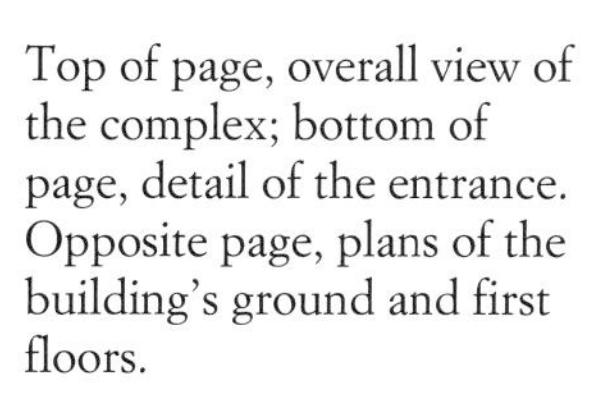

Top of page, overall view of the complex; bottom of page, detail of the entrance. Opposite page, plans of the building's ground and first floors.

COX CABLE
Parma, Ohio
1982

The client's objective was to create a functional, low budget building to enhance employee productivity and allow for rapid growth.
Located at the end of a cul-de-sac in an industrial park, the wooded six-acre site offered visual relief from the repetitive building design and vacant lots of other business establishments within the development. Maintaining the character of the site with its dense foliage and trees was a major design objective of both client and architect. The open gallery allows for staff to interact with others to gain a clear insight into the different roles, responsibilities and individuals involved in managing the process of cable television.

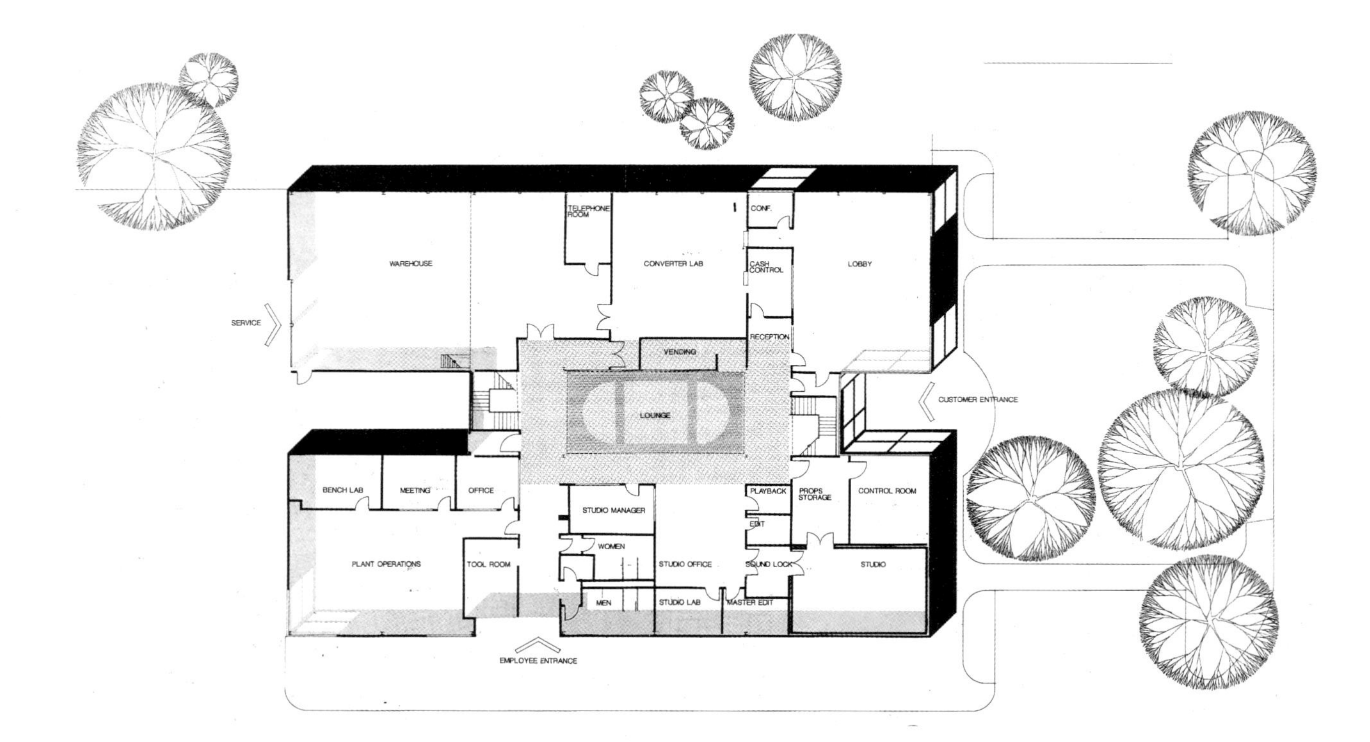

Interior view of the building showing its wide glass roof. Opposite page, plan.

A nighttime view of the building showing the interior lighting that emphasizes the interplay of glass walls.

SPAN THE TRACKS STUDY
University of Akron
Akron, Ohio
1984

The focus of the Study is a connecting axis which will bridge the gap between the University and downtown Akron, resulting in the addition of new facilities and renovation of existing structures. Master Planning focused on the organization of vehicle and pedestrian traffic, building location, space utilization and management studies for the Polymer Science Building, Community and Technological College, expanded Law School and other further educational facilities.
All the facilities are organized along a corridor of activities providing the opportunity for students and faculty to interact as they proceed from building to building.
The penetration of learning space within the downtown core provides for a new synergy in the urban center.
The selected location for the Polymer Science building, the expansion of the Law School, the new Business College, the retrofitting of the Polsky Building into the Community and Tech College reinforces the plan proposed in 1984. The Inventors Hall of Fame is also located along this axis. A new major artery will reinforce this connecting axis.

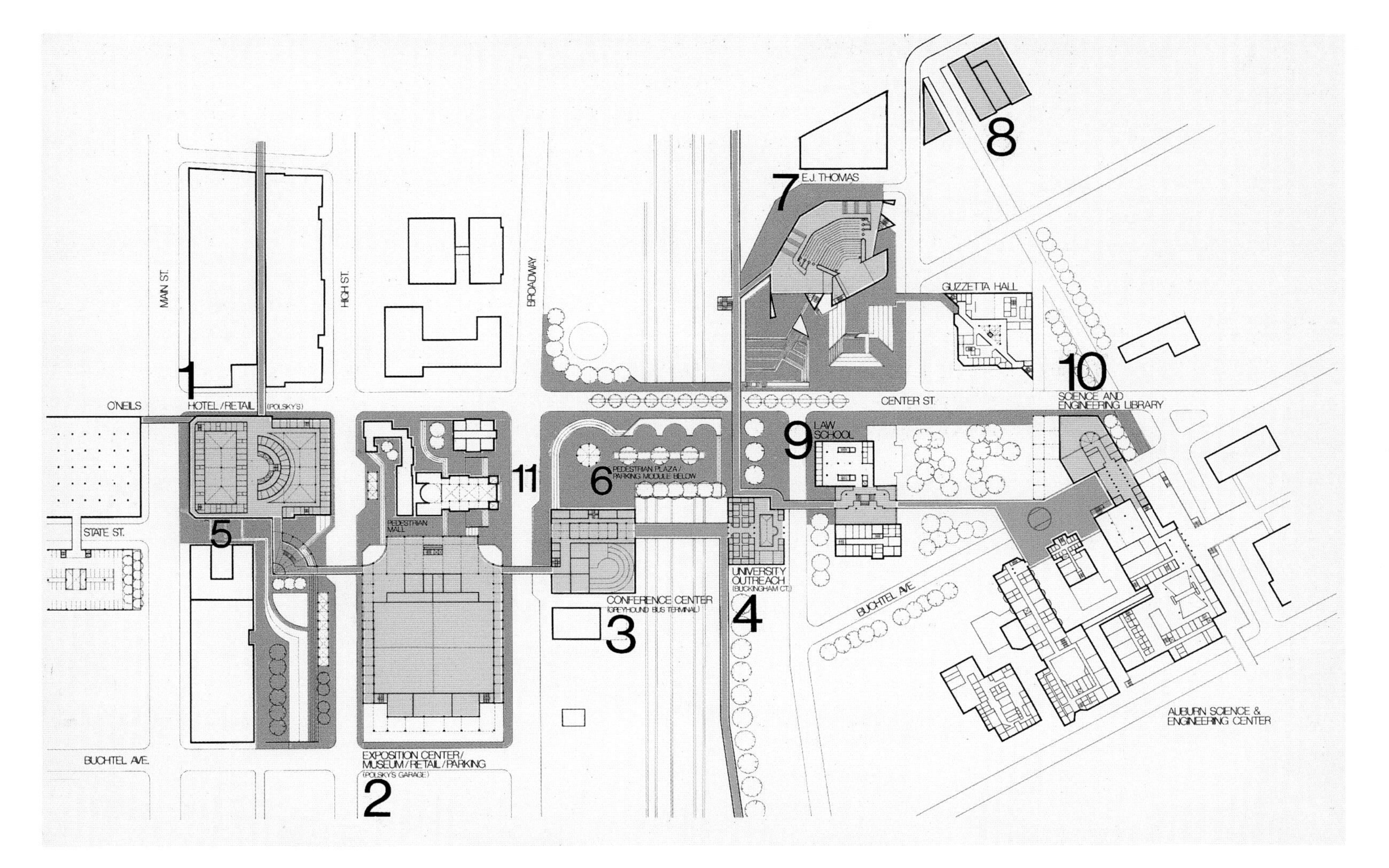

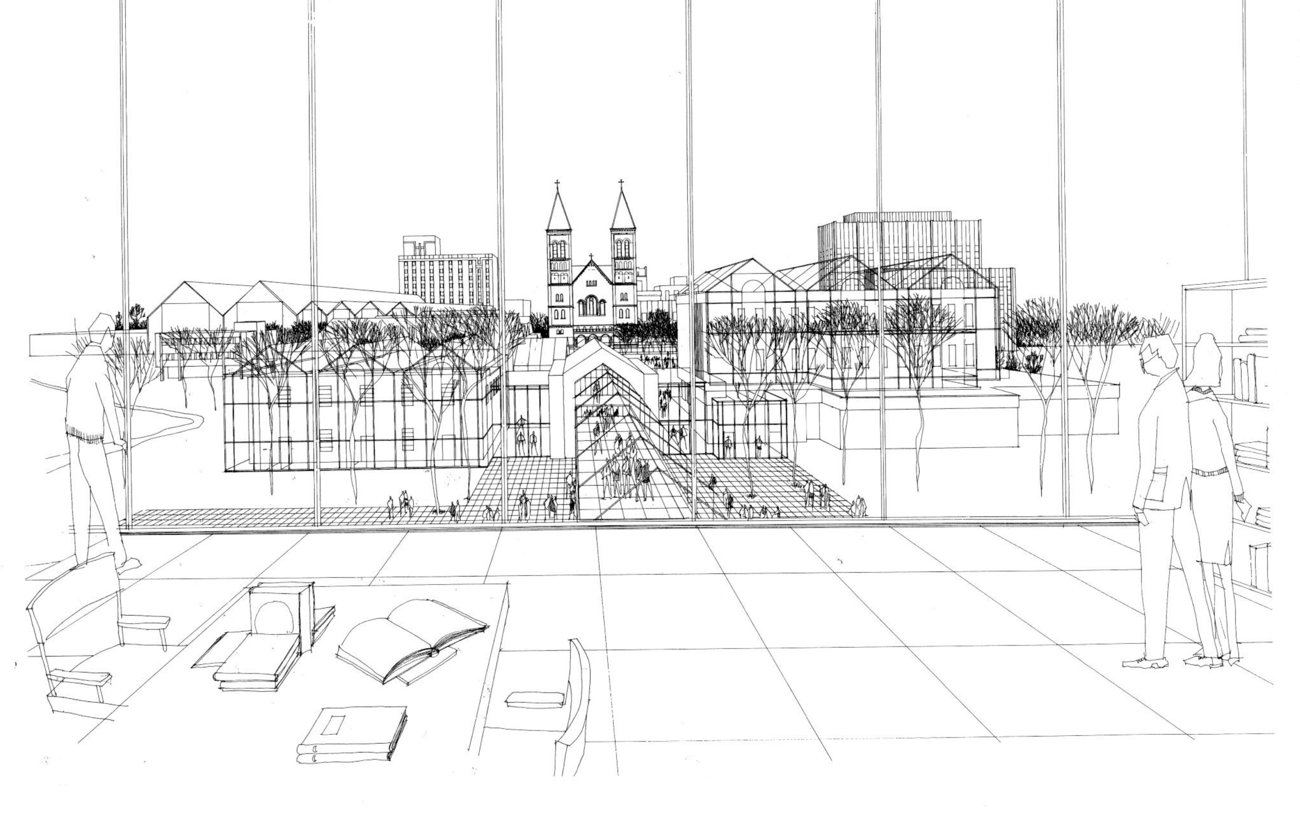

Site plan showing the layout of the urban services provided. Left, an axial view of one section of the urban project with the covered passage connecting all the facilities.

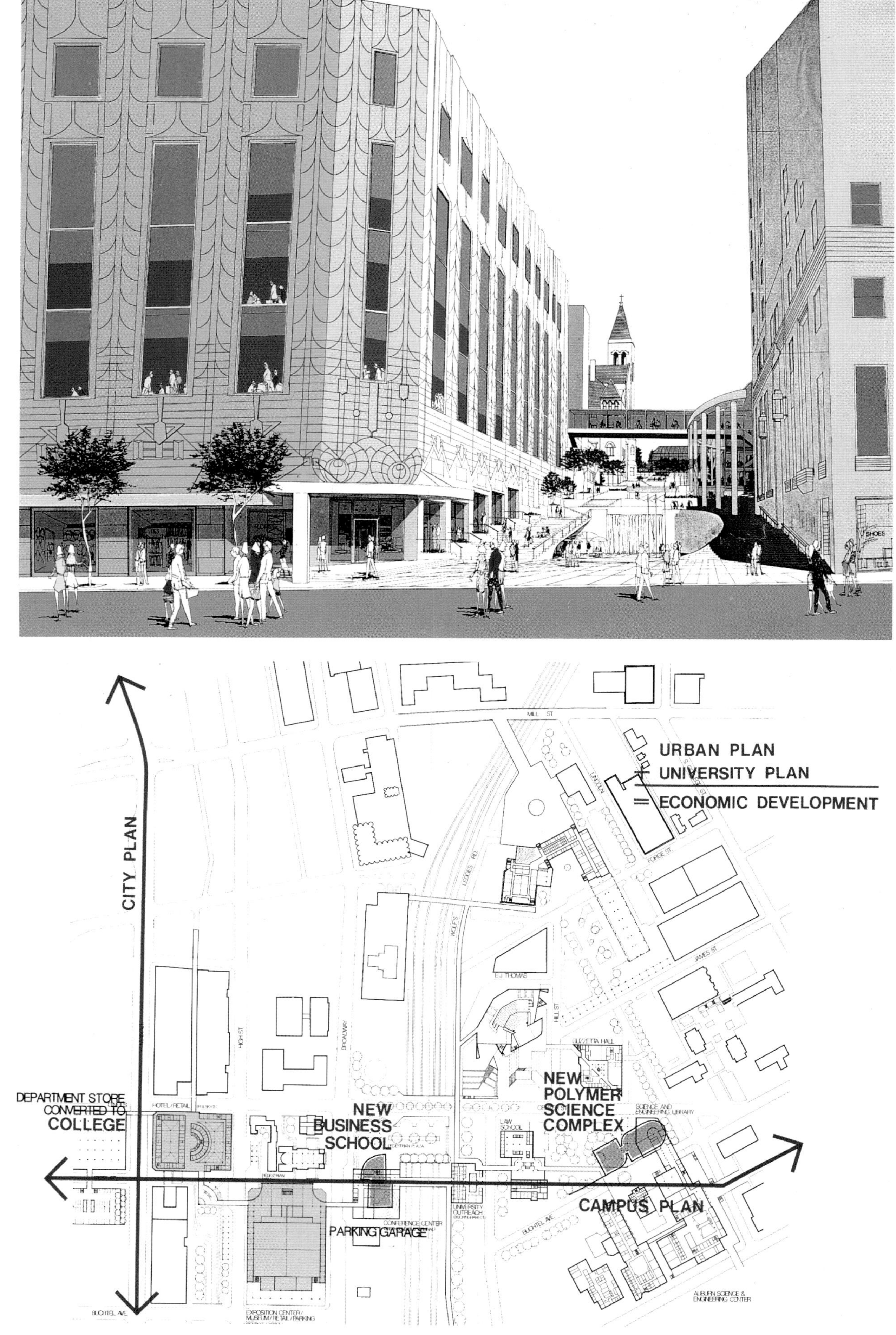

Perspective view of one of the project's focal points: the Polsky building, a departement store converted into college facilities.

Detailed plan of the university campus with the proposed additions.

Two views of the three-dimensional rendering of the entire project.

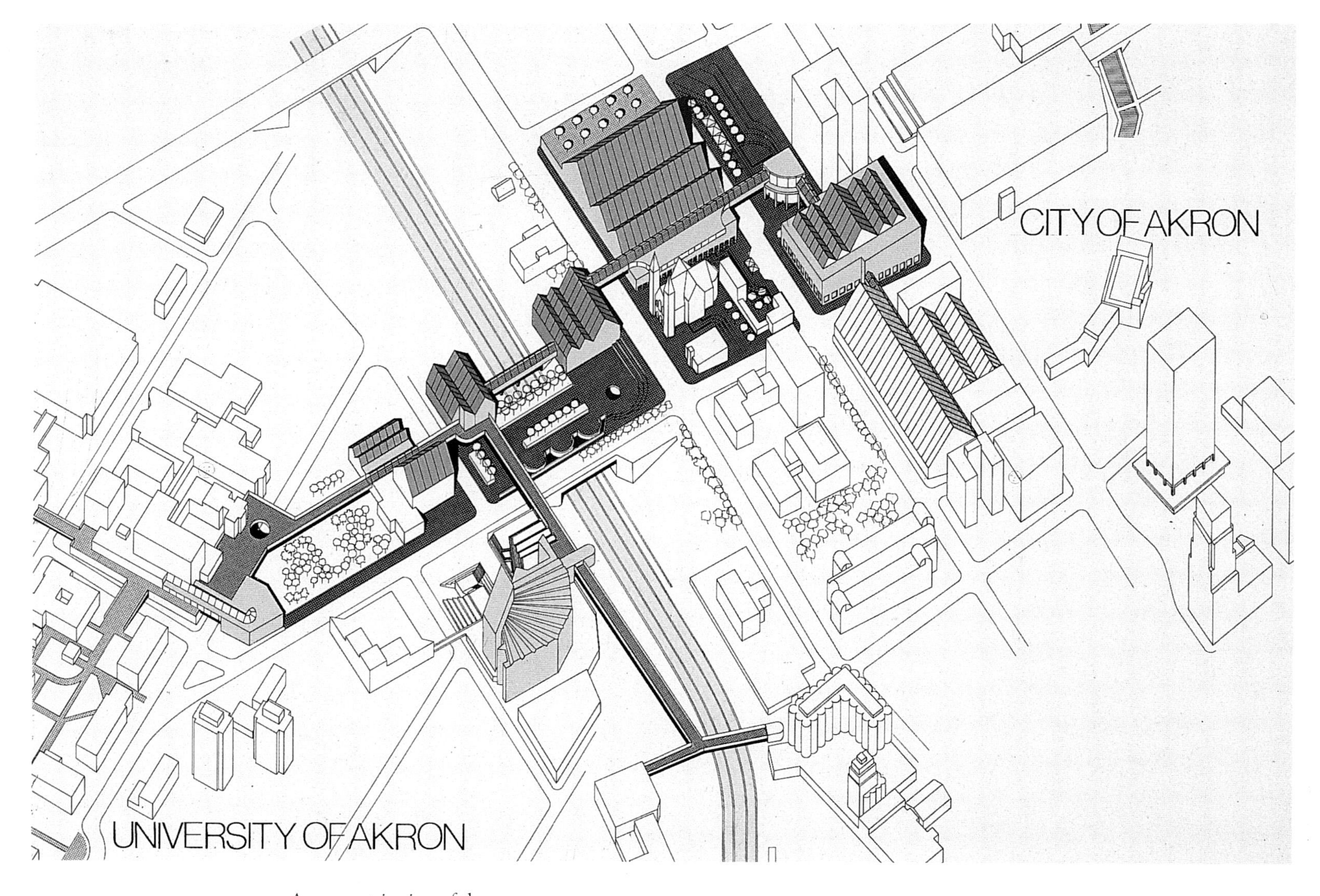

Axonometric view of the layout of the various facilities that will integrate university and urban realities.

Axial view of the three-dimensional rendering of the project.

MILLERSBURG CHURCH
Millersburg, Ohio
1984

This long-established rural congregation wished to leave its confining traditional structure in town and create a more serviceable facility in the open countryside.
A dramatically sloping site was chosen which offers a sweeping vista of the rolling countryside while affording high visibility from the nearby main route into town.
To accommodate a single-level plan and create a "sense of place," the hillside was mounded to form a circular plateau. This cleanly trimmed geometric podium contrasts with the natural contours and vegetation of the ten-acre site's remaining untouched area. The new church is situated on this platform to provide its major spaces with prime views. The locally quarried stone provides a visual base for the building.
The openness of this vista is echoed in the flow of spaces within the building. A central commons and fireplace provide a focal point around which the areas for worship, fellowship, education and administration are arranged. The silhouette of the building responds to these activities with common slopes of varying heights. In the administration and education areas, additional space was economically provided by constructing open-sided mezzanines beneath the roof peaks. The sanctuary has an exceptionally high peak creating a focus for the building's mass as viewed from the highway.
This compact, yet open center for worship, fellowship and education provides convenience, flexibility and room for growth in a dramatic new setting.

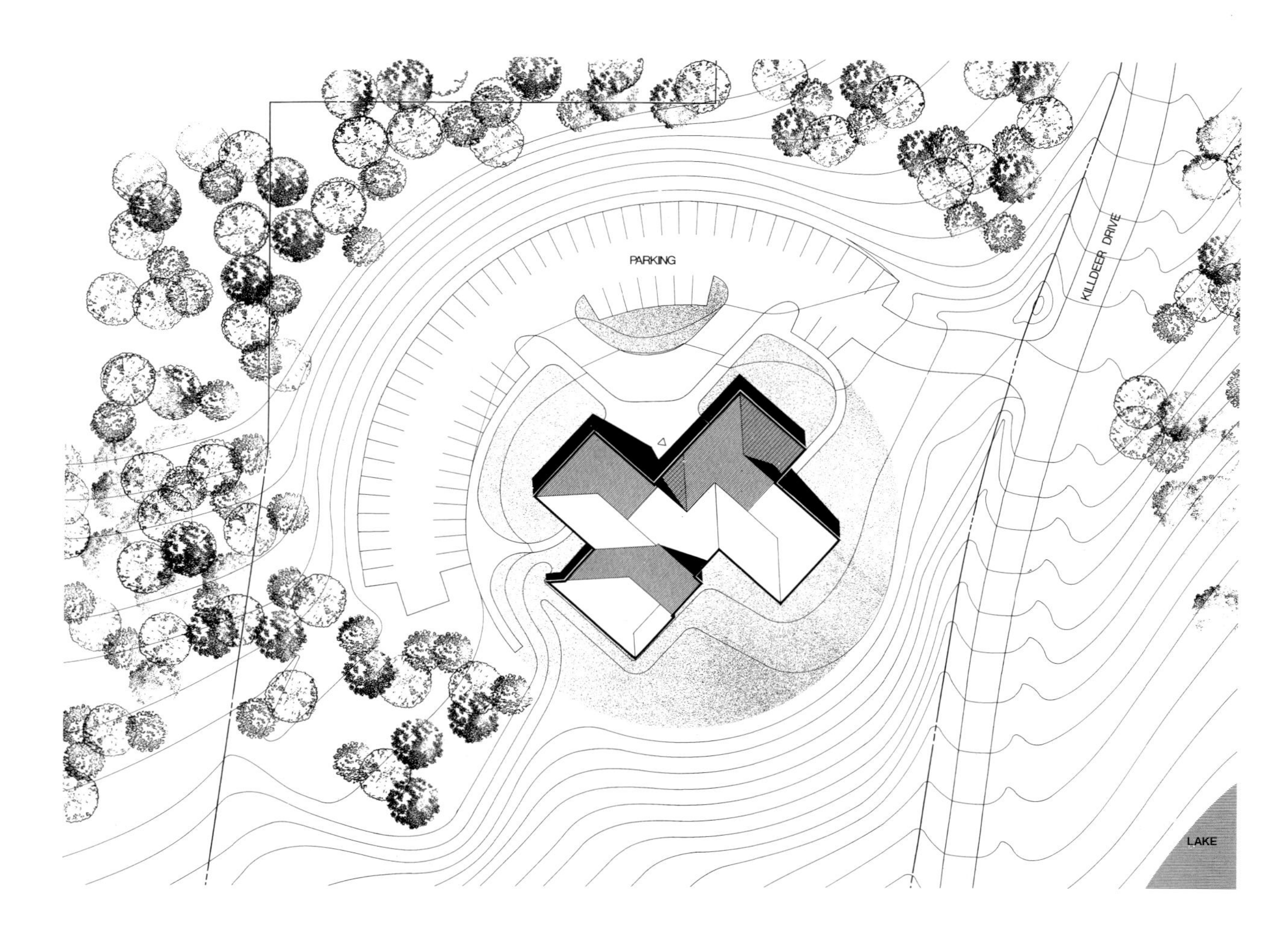

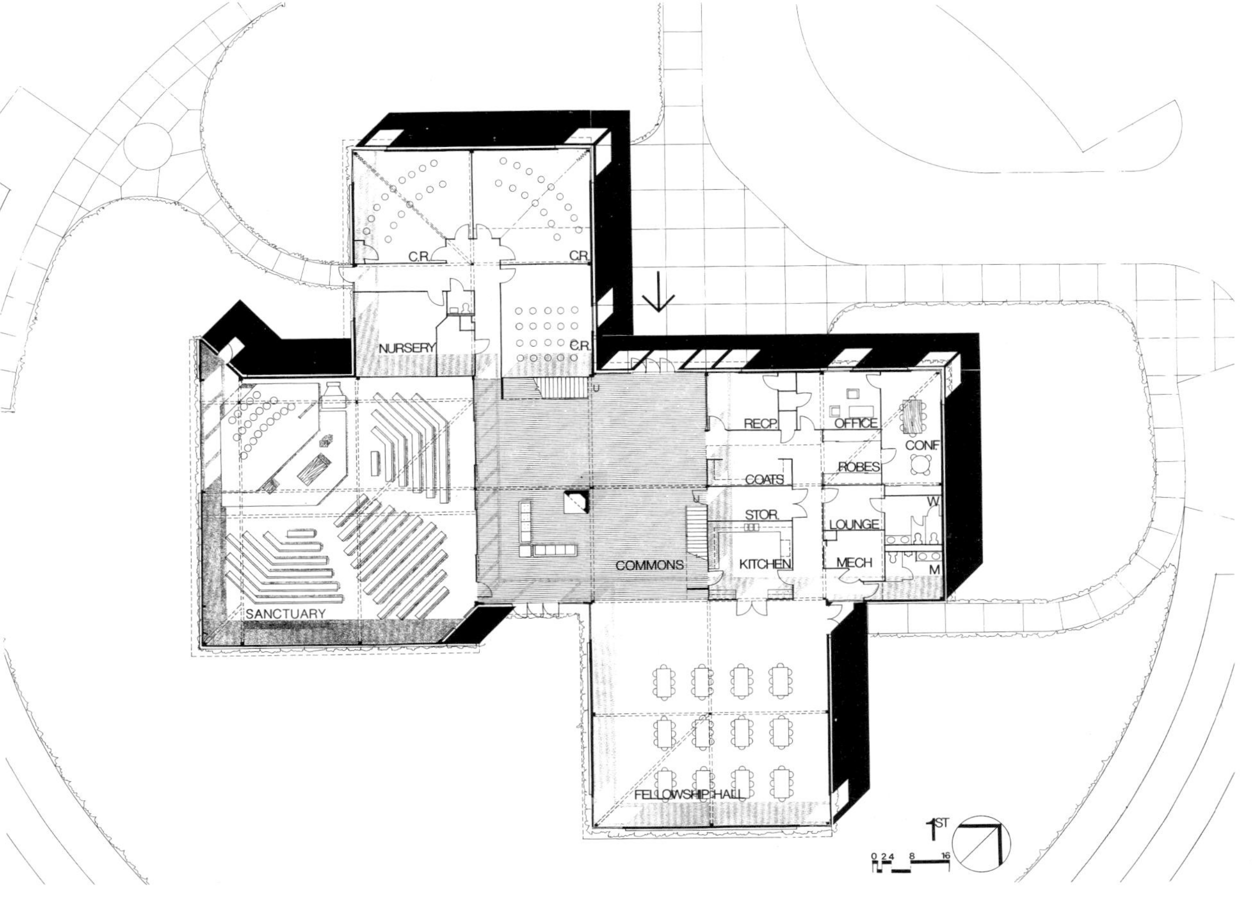

View of the building showing its intricate roof and plan showing the arrangement of fucntional space. Opposite page, site plan.

Interior of the sanctuary.

The exterior courtyard, and, below, the main facade with the entrance to the church.

STOW-MONROE FALLS HIGH SCHOOL
Stow, Ohio
1985

This facility, spatially defined by an innovative program, reflects the community's definition of an educational center for its entire constituency. Not only was the building to express an encyclopedia of learning, but it was also to instill excitement in the linkages that provide the cohesive character to the educational and cultural complex. Each volume of space was programmed, organized and conceptualized as a part of the whole. Requirements for secondary education were consistently supplemented to incorporate community educational opportunities.
Change is very apparent in the location of all program spaces organized along the circumference of a quarter circle. Early on, this was described as the critical conduit that the entire student body would use to reach all educational spaces. It is also referred to as the "Corridor of Action." All entrances and exits penetrate this space that is capable of accommodating the 1800 members of the student population.
This promenade/boulevard or bridge's purpose has been to inform or to accommodate many activities during the school day, evening hours, and weekends. Users can constantly be exposed to a variety of educational opportunities and are encouraged to participate. Every component that has been discovered and favorably evaluated has been incorporated in the building. It is a facility that demands response and encourages everyone to expand their own horizons, ultimately enriching the entire community.

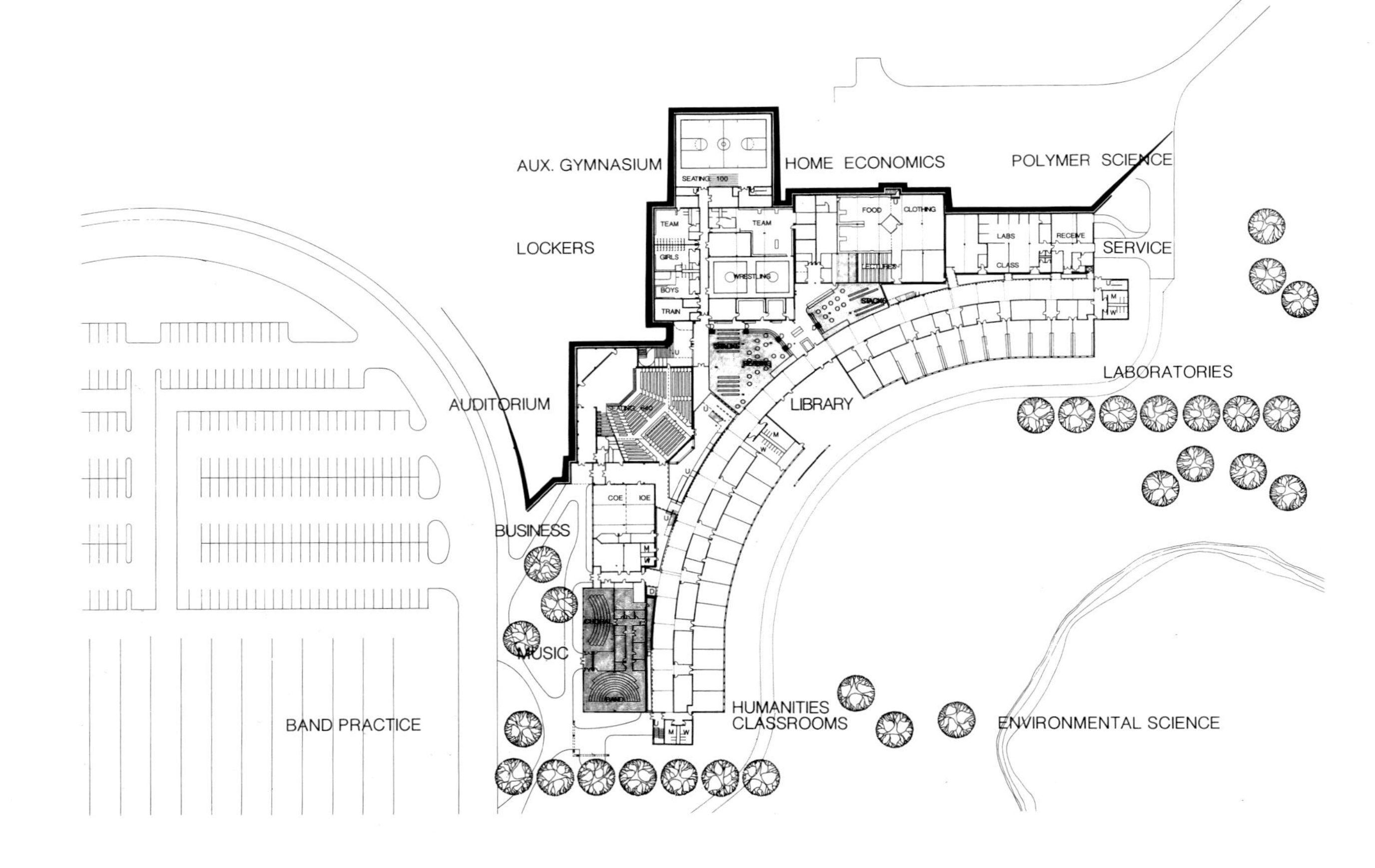

View of the finished project. Left, a picture of the model showing the building's unusal curved structure. Opposite page, lower level plan showing the arrangement of functional spaces.

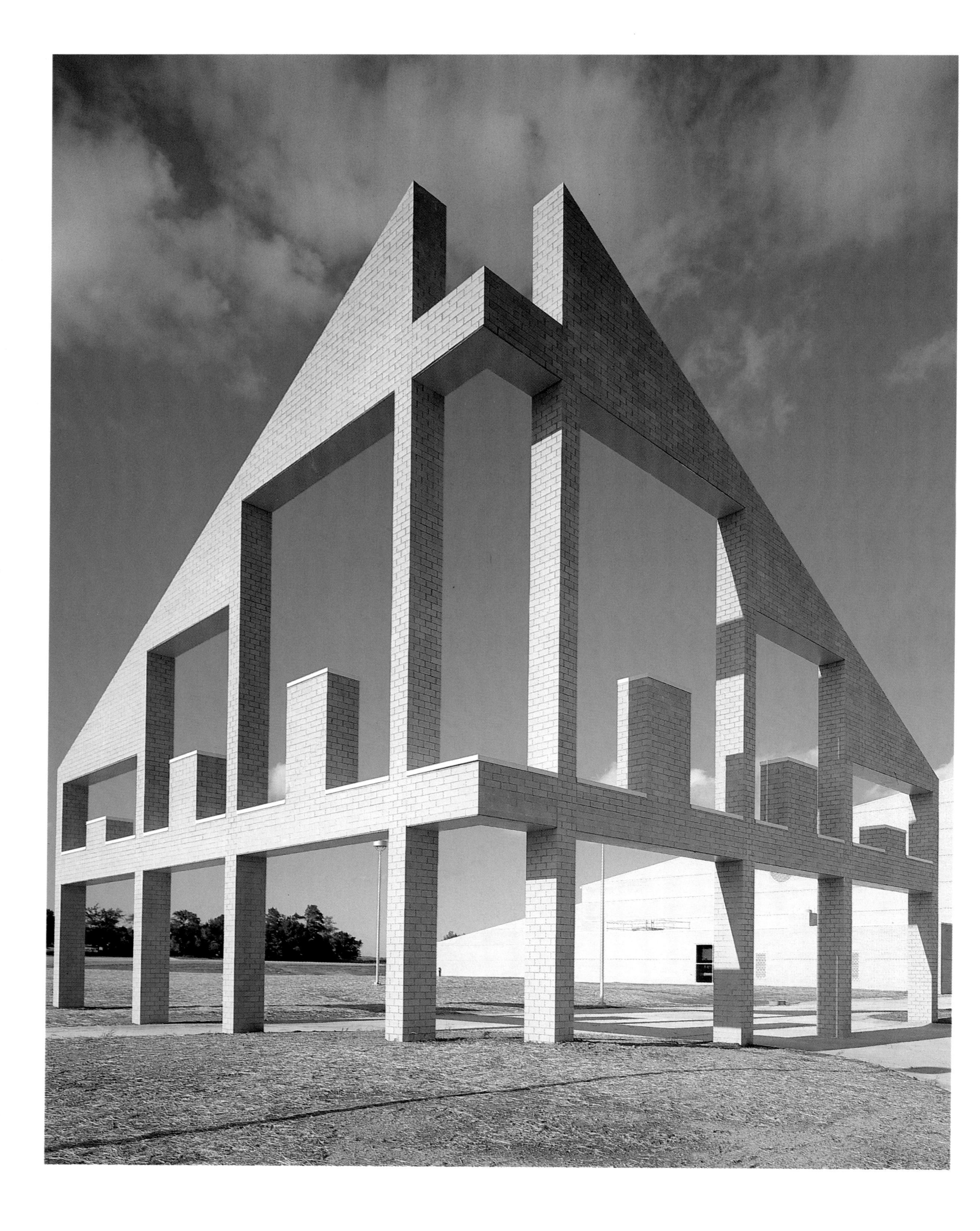

This long-distance view of the building highlights its smooth integration into the environment. Opposite page, the symbolic wall marking the entrance area of the school.

Interior view of the complex
with the stairs and ramps
connecting the articulate
sections of the building.

Another detail of the composite architectural structure.

COMMUNITY SCHOOL
Seattle, Washington
1986

Lake Washington school district decided to build an innovative high school in the rapidly expanding and densely populated heart of the community were investigated.
As a part of the initial analysis a variety of planning options were investigated where the image of the building would play an important role in creating a signature for this part of the Seattle area. One alternative that captured the imagination of the School Board was the proposal to provide a community school within the geometric form of a pyramid.
The planning process logically located the gymnasium and performing arts area on the ground floor approximately 10 feet below existing grade. The administration was located on the periphery of the ground level with Humanities and the visual arts on the second or third levels. A multi-level library media center providing an abundance of information for research independent learning and a tutorial approach to the process of teaching was located in the center of the new school.
Even though this particular project created a great deal of tension the final design was based along more traditional lines and a more conventional educational curriculum.

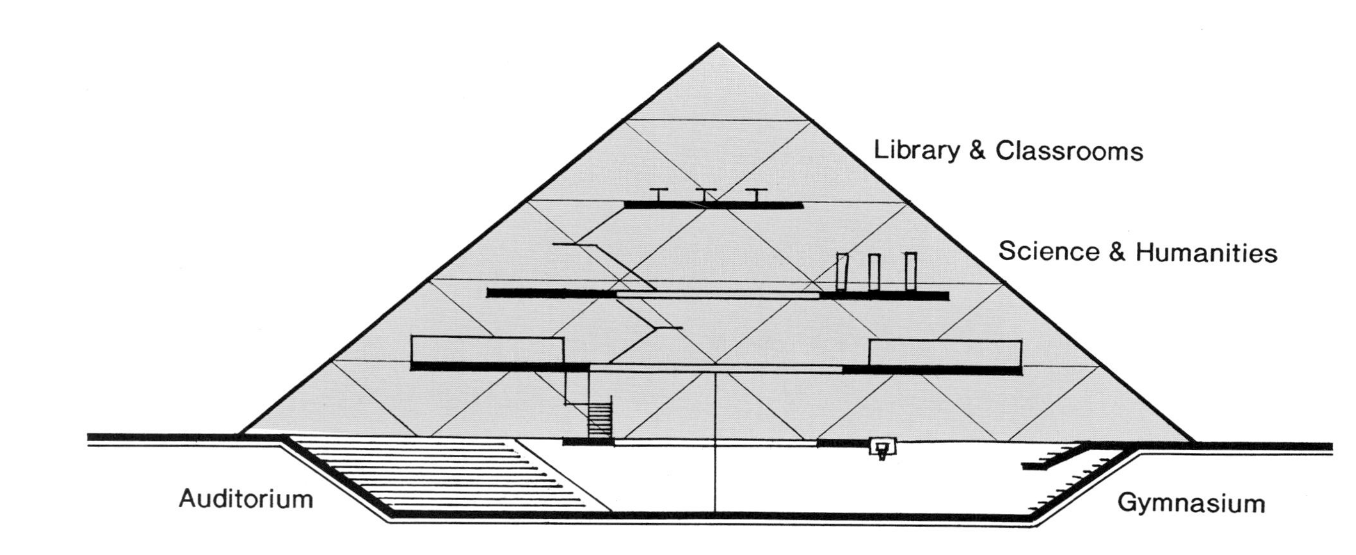

View of the model.
Opposite page and below, section and plan of the building.

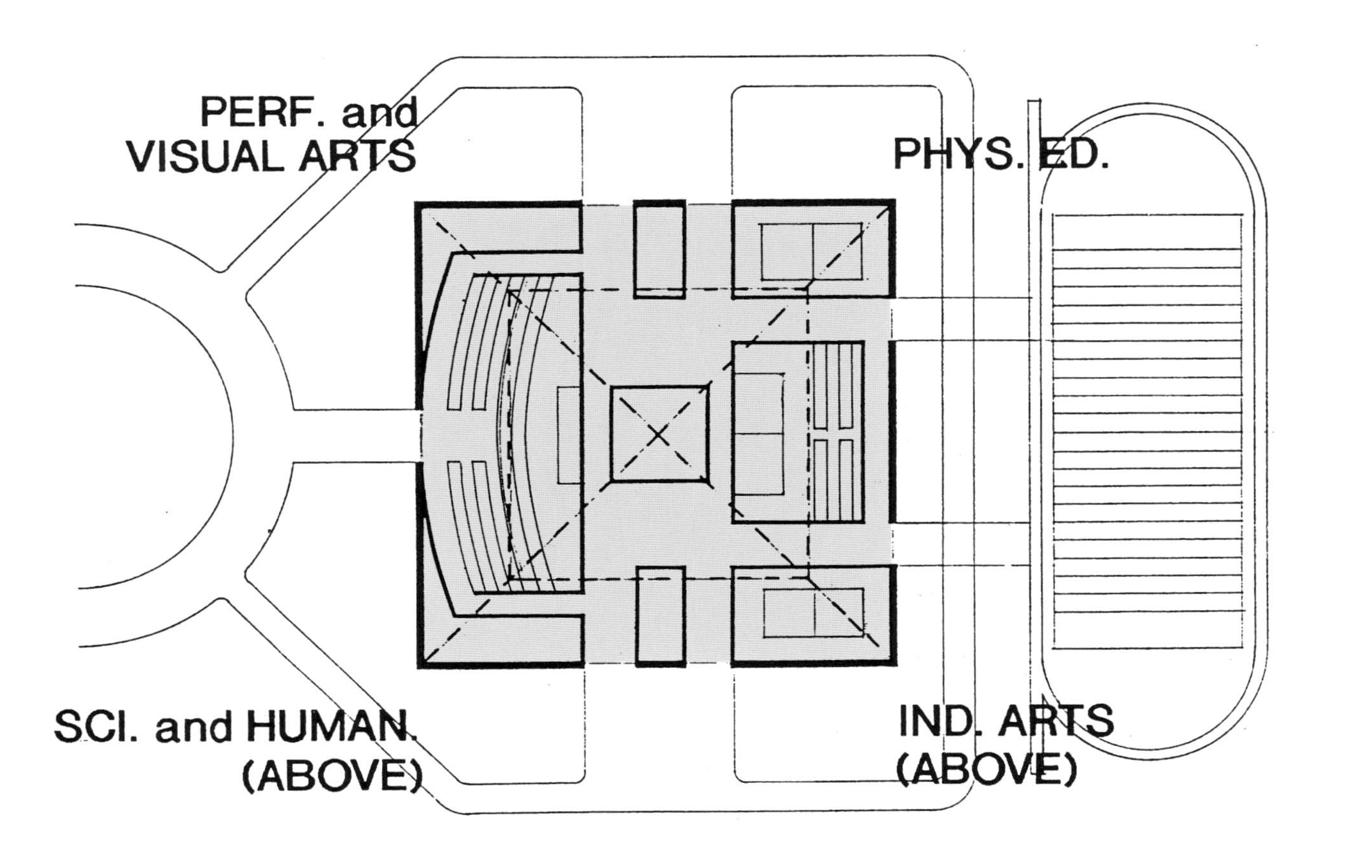

ONTARIO-HURON CENTER
Cleveland, Ohio
1987

The Ontario Center, a proposed corporate office structure, will be a significant addition to Cleveland's growing skyline, as well as occupying a significant position along the gateway to the downtown area. It is important that the building should reflect the opportunity presented by its location.

The concept involves a unique shape that reflects the dimensions of its site. A curving facade going from south to west and roof that slopes up from south to north seem to draw people up into the heart of downtown Cleveland along Ontario Street.

The building is clad entirely in transparent and opaque glass, reflecting sunlight during the day and glowing, fully illuminated, animated with life and energy at night. The 25,000 sq. ft. floor plate allows for maximum flexibility. However, the dimensional measurements of the top 20 to 27 floors allow for two unique solutions to the problem.

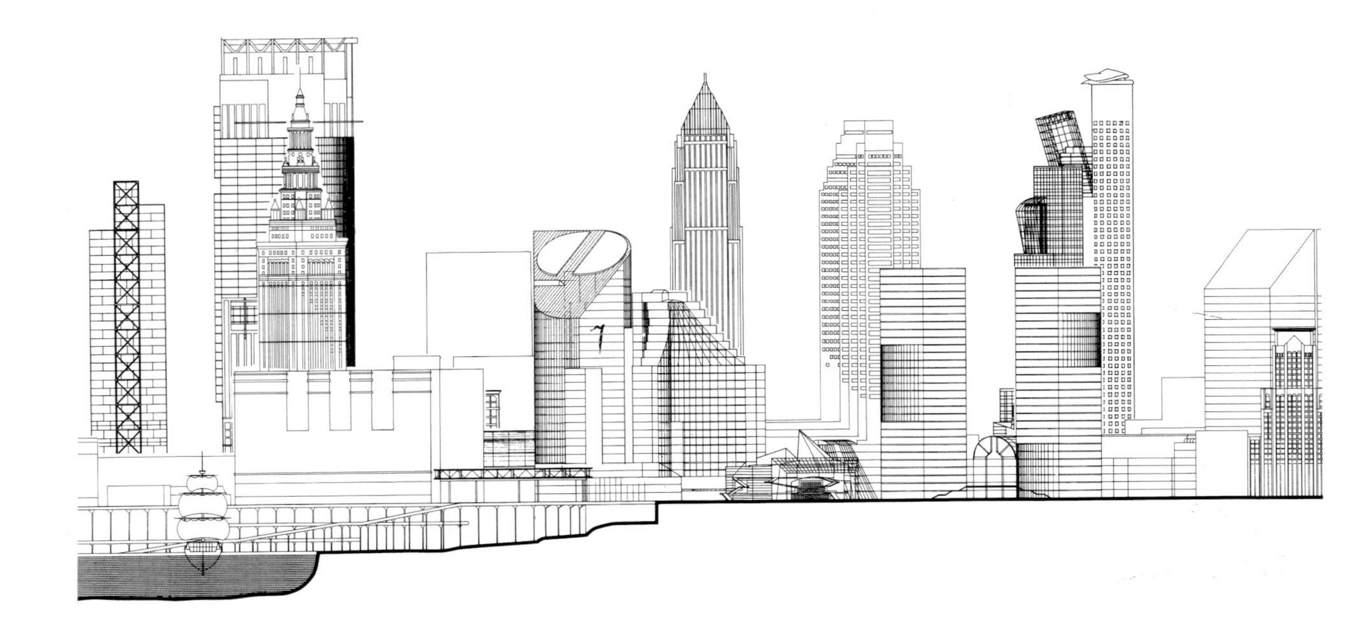

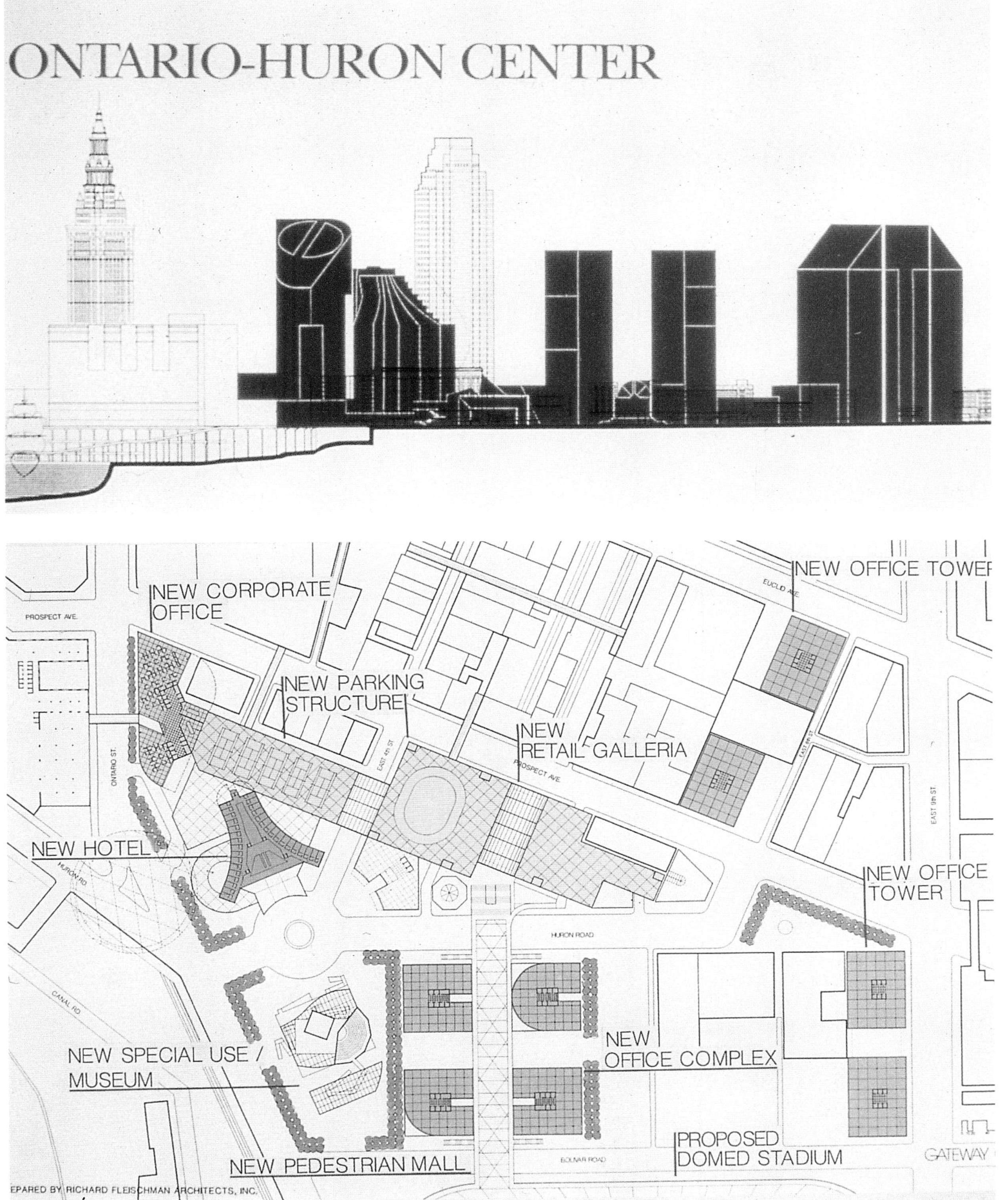

A general view of the planned buildings and their territorial location.

Site plan showing the arrangement of spaces and functions. Opposite page, elevation of the urban area around the project site, showing how the new buildings have been incorporated in the surrounding architectural fabric.

Overall view of the model of the urban development project.

Detail of the model highlighting the architectural quality of the planned constructions.

Two views of the main tower showing the complex's potentiality of becoming a distinctive architectural landmark on the cityscape.

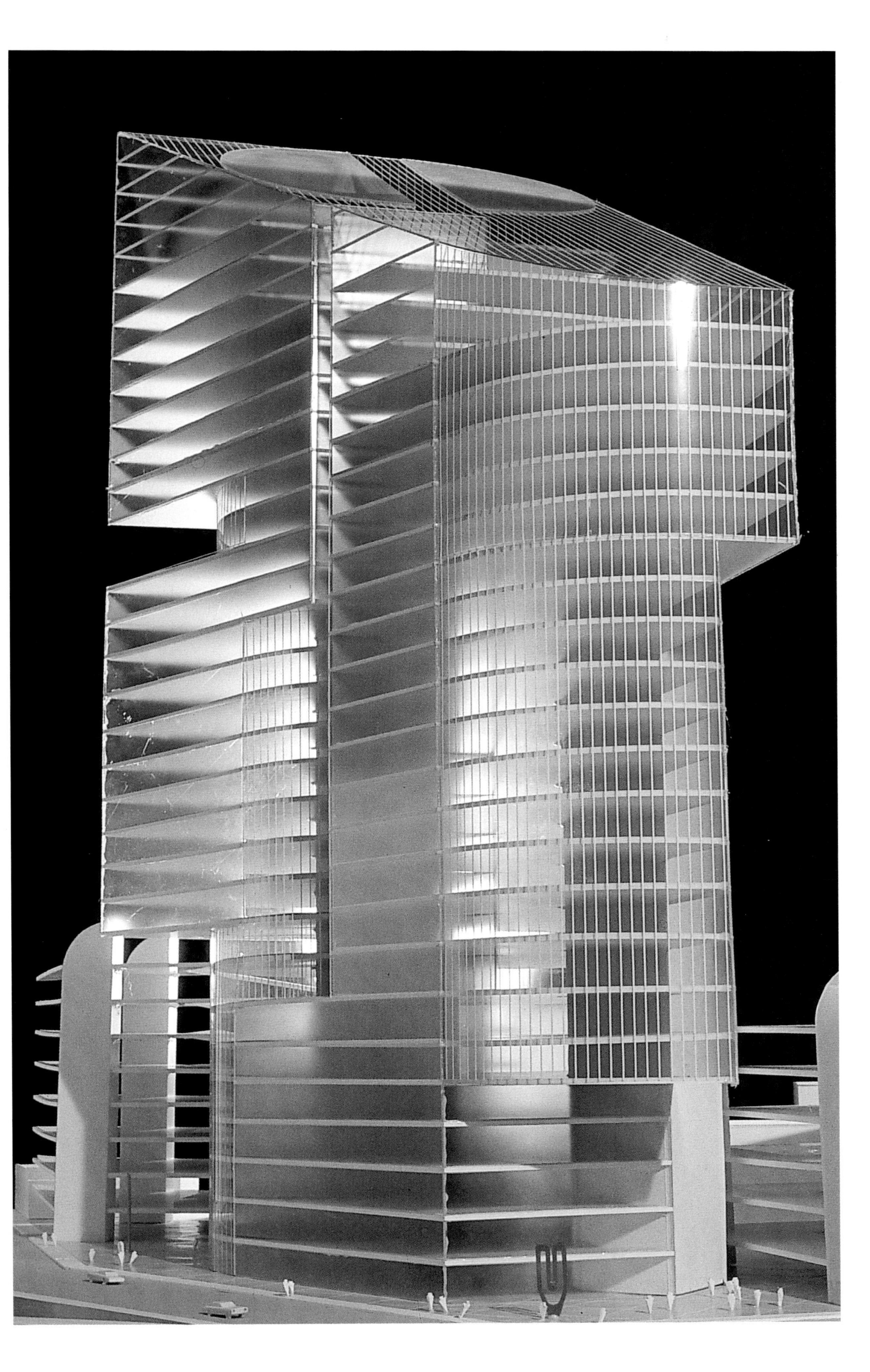

MOUNTAINLAIR STUDENT UNION BUILDING
WEST VIRGINIA UNIVERSITY
Morgantown, West Virginia
1989

Mountainlair is located at the center of the downtown campus of the West Virginia University in Morgantown.
A series of evaluations indicated that the following feasible programmatic changes would need to be implemented: expanded dining space from an existing capacity of 1,000 to 1,500 or more to accommodate increasing market opportunities; provisions for ten to twelve specialized food vendors, which may be run by franchised operators or by the Mountainlair staff; assure the continued operation of Mountainlair's Buffeteria, providing a single choice, nutritionally balanced menu; encourage more students to use the dining area more frequently by providing appropriate entertainment; add ten meeting and conference rooms with food service options, as well as space for student organizations; improve circulation and access for the handicapped.
The renovation and addition will facilitate student movement through the building, providing easy access to its various activities, as well as creating a sense of celebration for students and faculty.
A new sense of openness is created by a revised spatial organization at the center of the building.
The additional dining space has been provided by filling in the small plaza defined by the parking structure. The resulting space, with the mezzanine and bridges connecting it to the second floor, created an ideal area for entertainment and congregation. Mountainlair is a 15,000-square-foot renovation.

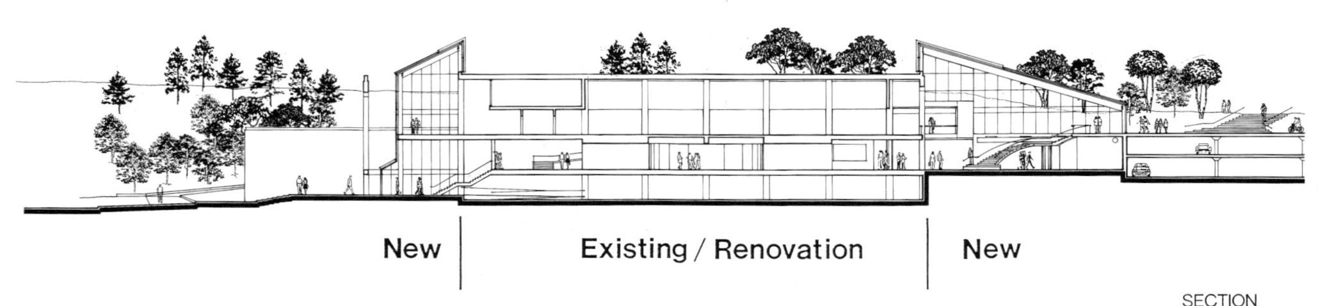

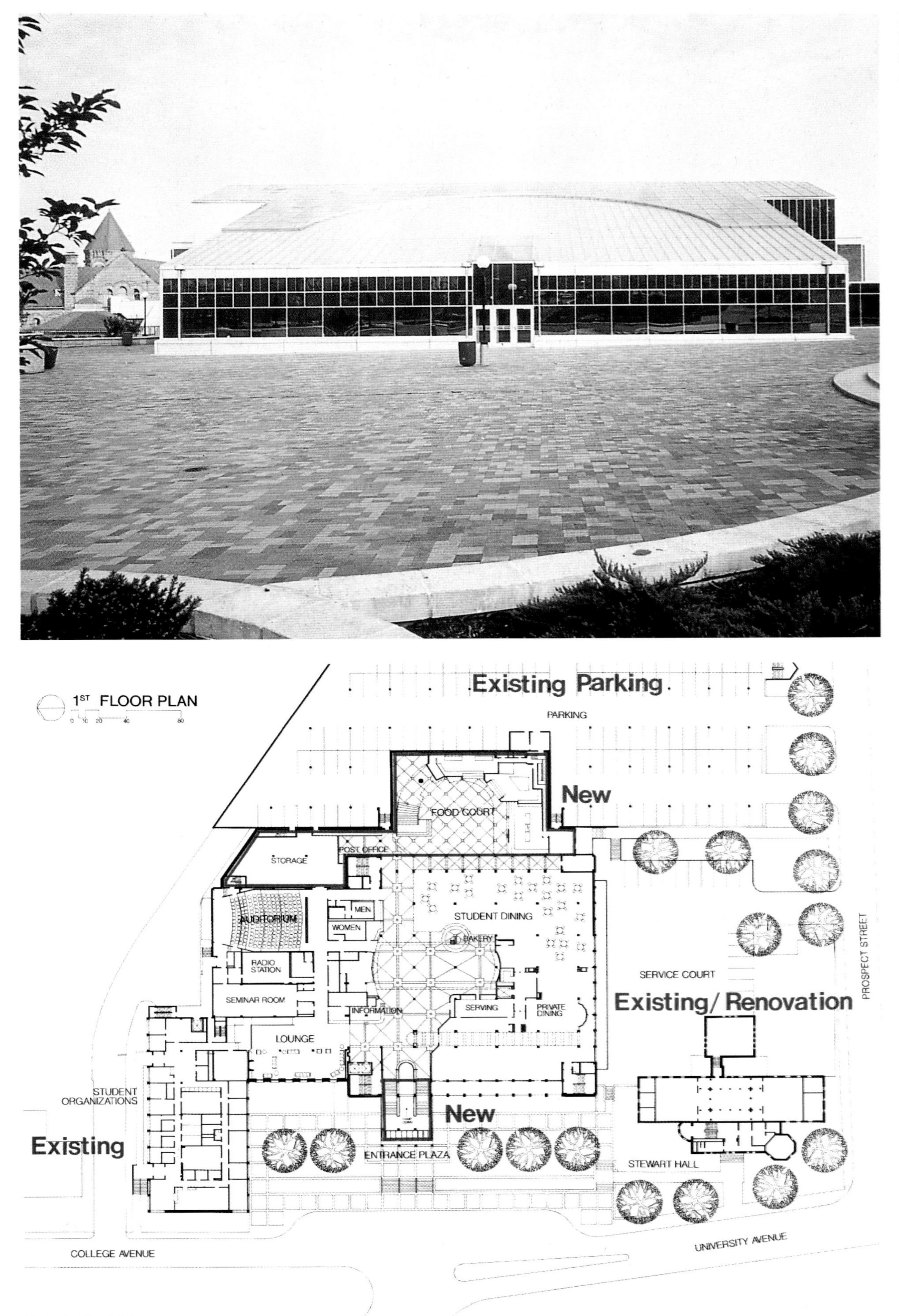

Main facade of the new building and first floor plan. Opposite page, cross section of the whole complex.

External view of the new entrance hall facing the entrance plaza.

External and internal views of the new wing designed to expand the dining and meeting areas. The sloping roof covers the entry to the new food court.

STUDIO OF RICHARD FLEISCHMAN ARCHITECTS, INC.
Cleveland, Ohio
1989

The Dodd Camera Building located at 1025 Huron Road was retrofitted to accommodate Richard Fleischman Architects' studio.
The entire building was reduced to the base structure. The result was a flexible openness that was conducive to the peculiar management style of an architecture practice.
Sculpting a variety of spaces by opening up the floor areas as well as the roof structure provided additional openness that facilitated communication between the three floors of activity. Subtle additions such as spiral stairs and a skylight complemented the open feeling, allowing a logical flow of movement and light to complement the goals of the firm.

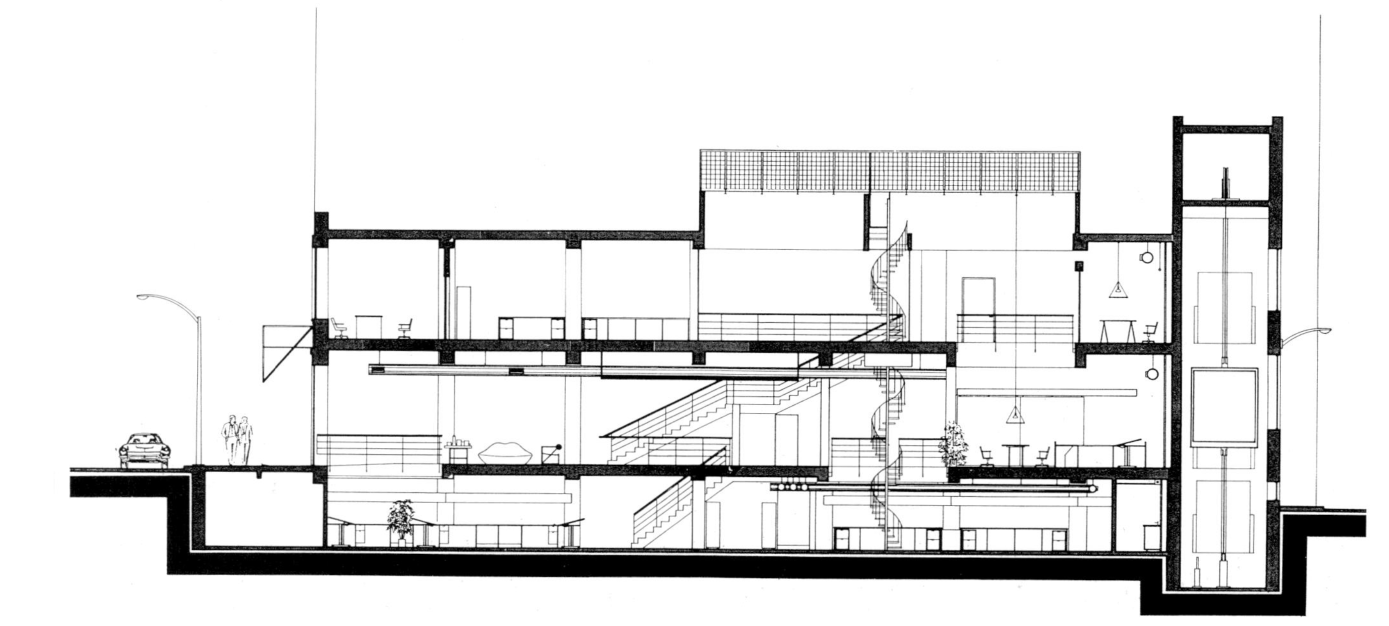

Interior view of the studio with the conference hall and, opposite page, section of the building.

Plans of the various levels of the studio.

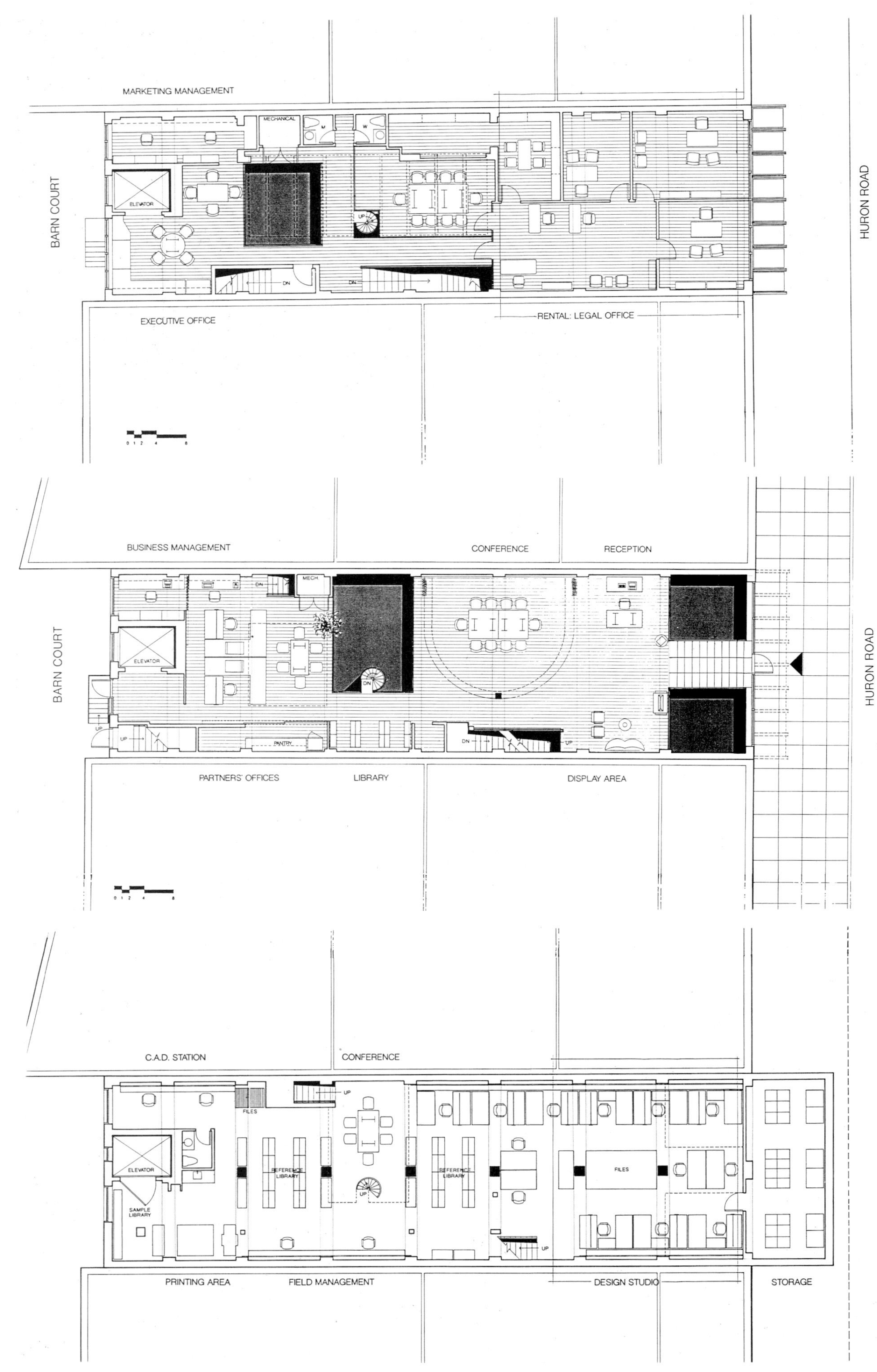

An interior of the business management area.

COLLEGE OF ENGINEERING NITSCHKE HALL
UNIVERSITY OF TOLEDO
Toledo, Ohio
1989

The project is to retrofit an existing industrial research complex acquired by the University of Toledo in order to expand the College of Engineering.
In 1989 it was the intent of this institution to reorganize the entire 250,000-square-foot existing building for all disciplines taught at the College. Program Analysis and Space Utilization studies resulting in cost comparisons indicated that this strategy was not economical. Careful scrutinization of the program, space, and cost data indicated that an alternate strategy would be advisable. Therefore, 100,000 square feet or one-third of the open industrial structure was converted into civil, mechanical and electrical engineering laboratories. A new structure for civil, chemical and industrial laboratories was built as a major addition along with 75,000 square feet of faculty and graduate assistant offices, and classroom and lecture facilities. The bids received on June 22, 1993 were substantially below the estimate.
The blending of the two structures, existing and new, provided new educational opportunities for all engineering disciplines, as well as a new image for an expanding educational program for engineering. The retrofitting of the existing research complex was accomplished by creating a series of commons that mark the College's new entrance.
The new five-story office tower attempts to incorporate some of the qualities of the existing building while introducing new technological components in the now one-story building. Open multi-level spaces provide seminar activities for the different engineering disciplines. The use of open stairways provides convenient access to different departments and encourages interaction between the entire engineering community. The solution is simple and the plan reflects the clarity of organization of the parts that appear to blend into one single concept.
A major component of Nitschke Hall is an auditorium/lecture hall that seats 200 and provides an audio-visual environment that encourages conferences and communications as an integral part of the teaching space.

The two facades of the building showing the intricate layout of volumes.

Ground and first floors plans showing the focal points of the project.

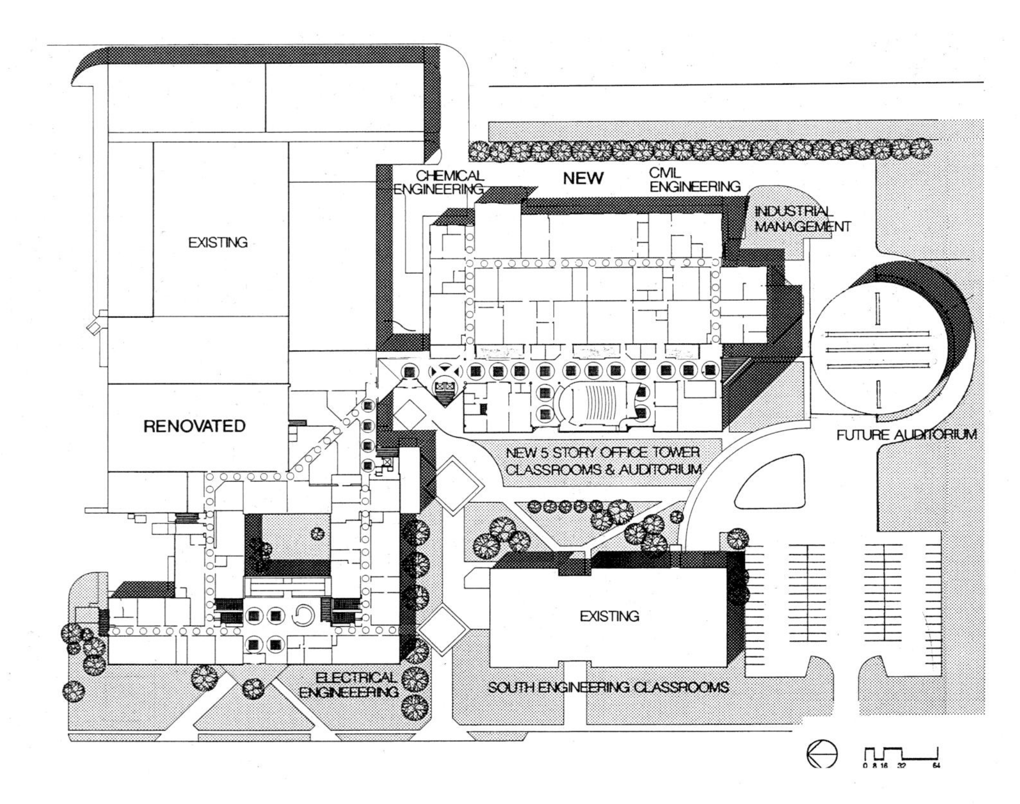

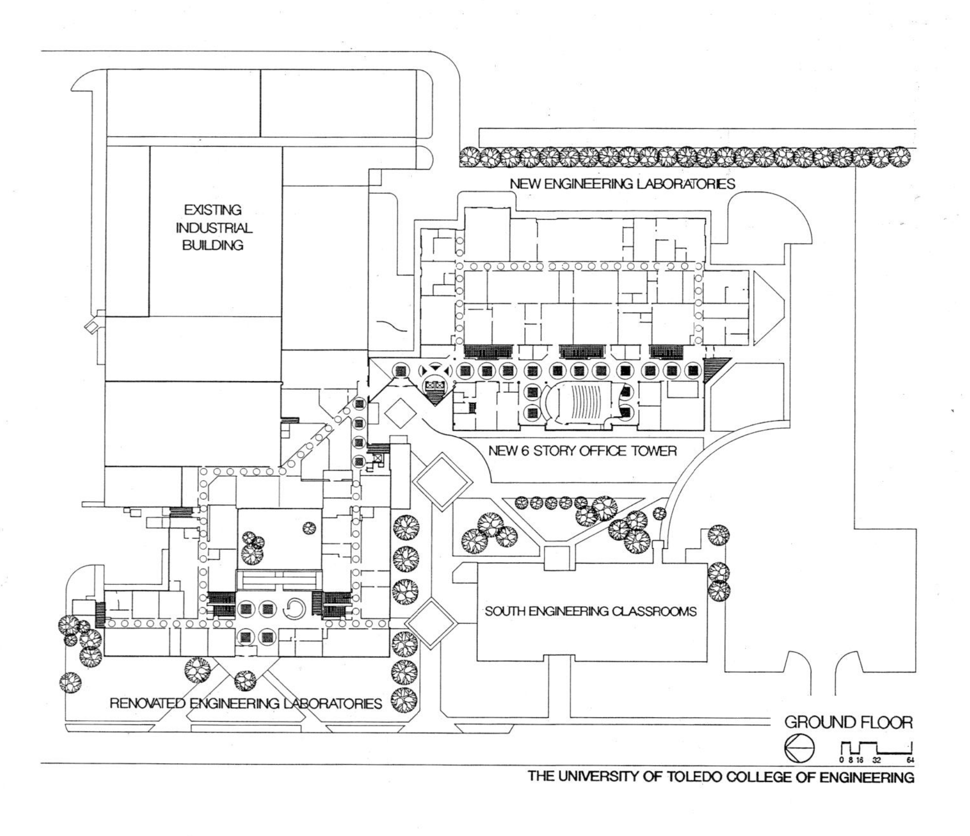

The trasparent glass tower which contains service stairs and others technical equipments.

NORTH COAST HARBOR DEVELOPMENT DESIGN GUIDELINES/MASTER PLAN
Cleveland, Ohio
1990

The North Coast Harbor represents economic and irreplaceable public assets as the largest developable lake front site in downtown Cleveland, offering the community a unique opportunity. The potential for economic growth inherent with this major development is such that all developments proposed for the area will be held to the highest standard of design.

The development program for the project anticipates a large scale mixed-use development comprised of major public attractions, public open space, retail, office, hotel, parking and residential facilities. Collectively, this combination of elements will work together to create a synergistic, vibrant environment where people can live, work, shop and enjoy cultural and recreational attractions.

The concept proposed attempts to promote the highest and best use of the site, and to create a development with outstanding visual quality. Steel and cable structures which are so characteristic of the Great Lakes industrial vernacular, reflect a tradition in the design expression throughout the complex. The Master Plan is to accommodate the Rock & Roll Hall of Fame, Great Lakes Museum and other commercial and retail developments.

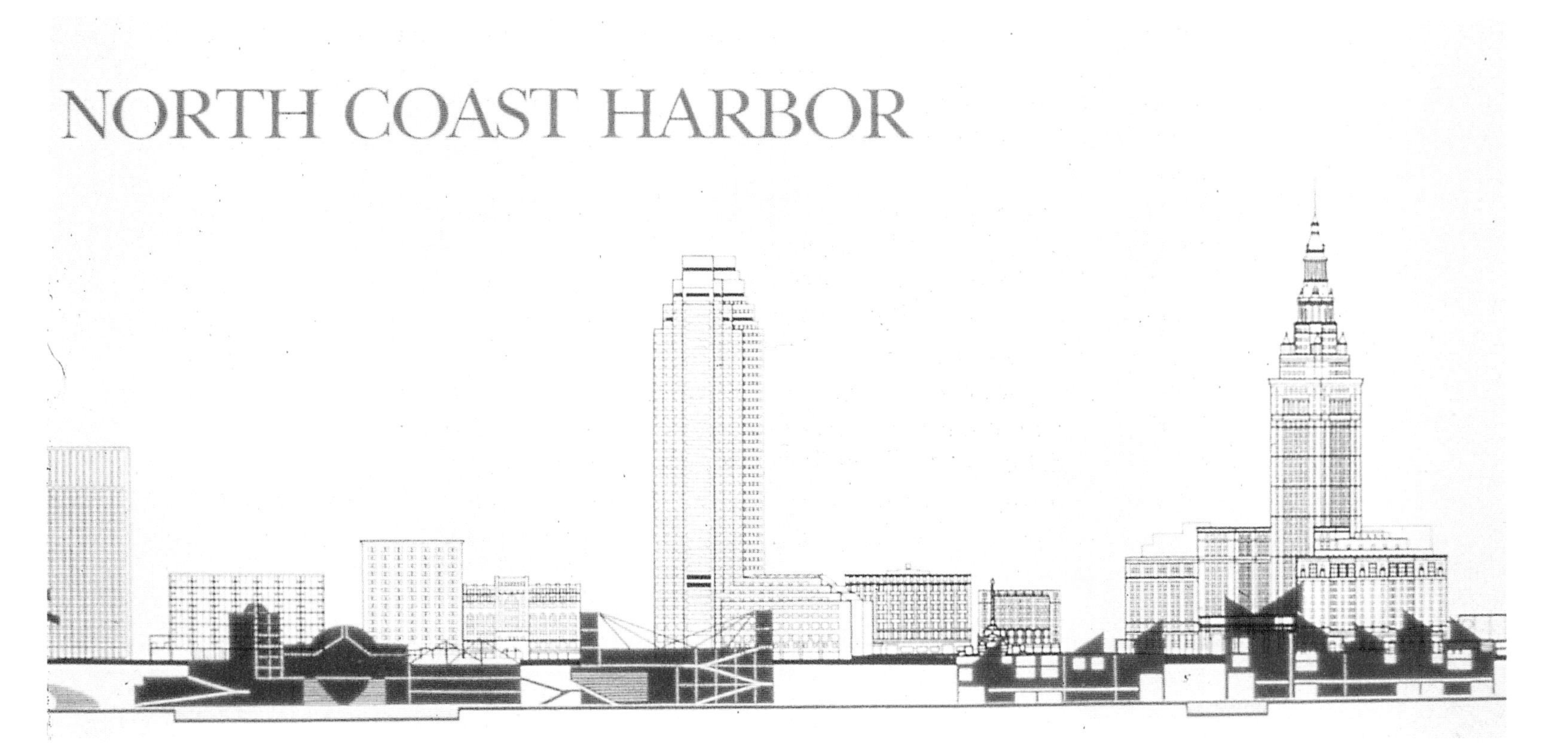

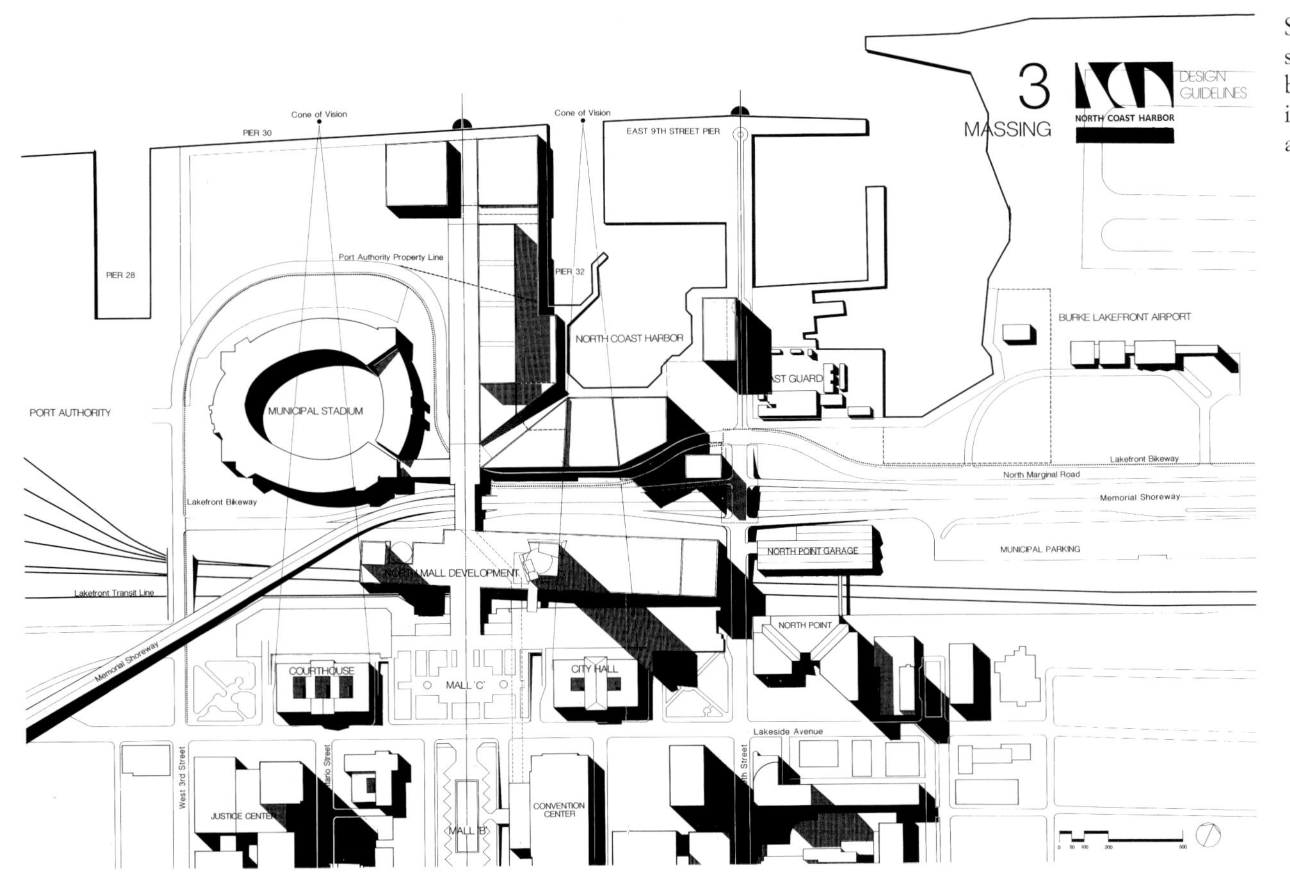

Section and site plan showing how the new buildings will be incorporated in the existing architectural context.

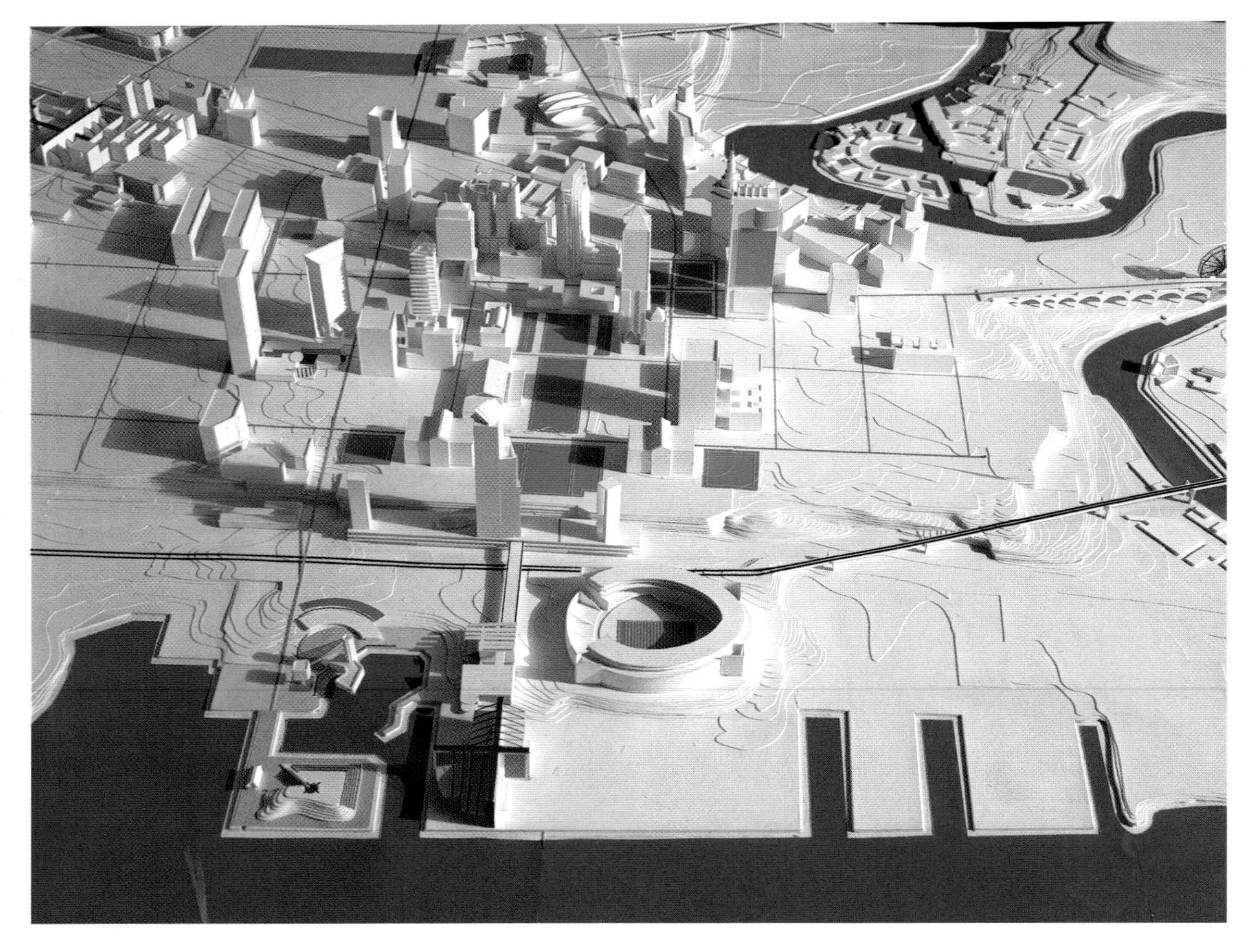

Overall view of the model.

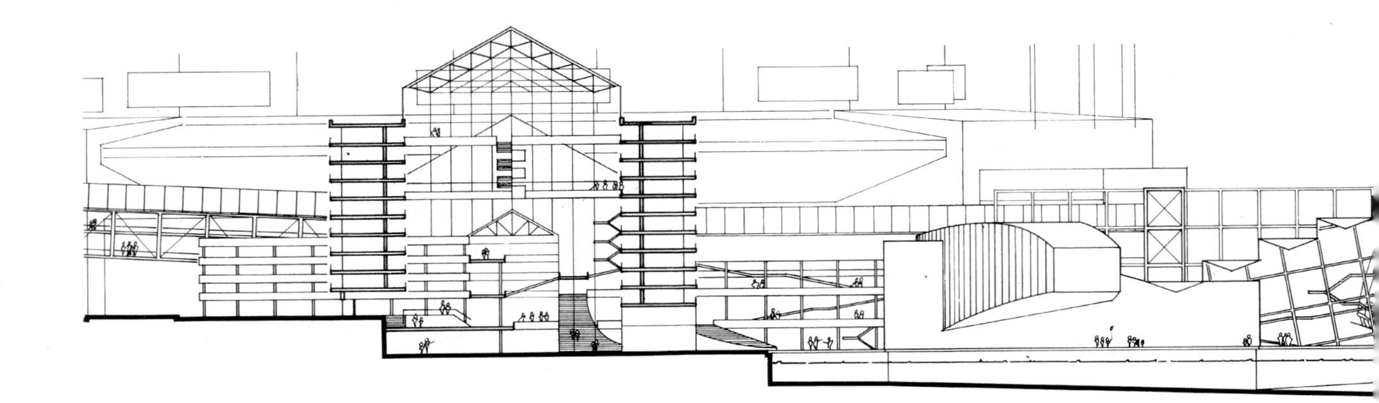

Perspective view and, below,
section of the proposed
lakefront.

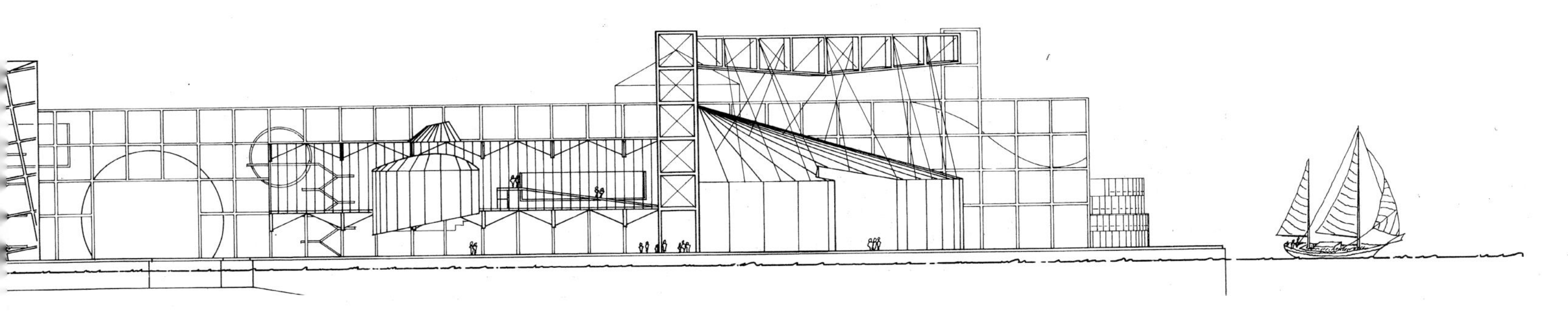

CONVENTION PLAZA
HOTEL OFFICE RETAIL COMPLEX
Cleveland, Ohio
1990

The Convention Plaza is a mixed-use development that includes an office building, hotel, retail, and parking garage to be located on two major intersections in downtown Cleveland. The unique consolidation of an office building, hotel and parking garage, each positioned over the next, provides the kind of silhouette associated a signature building. This comprehensive program includes a 615,200-square-foot structure (with 23 floors of office space) architecturally balanced on a podium of 16 floors, eleven of which accommodate 416 hotel guestrooms and meeting facilities. The 1,000-space parking garage completes the base and supplies the necessary on-site parking required for a complex of this magnitude. The juxtaposition of the Office Tower over the linear-shaped Hotel creates a dramatic architectural relief in the exterior facade that compliments the urban scale of this major glass-sheeted structure.
The entire building complex is planned to be made of structural steel, fire-proofed, and enclosed in various shades of glass, a proportion of which will be opaque. Granite, mainly on the ground floor, is also incorporated in specific areas of the building. The reflective quality of glass will mirror the many fine architectural buildings contiguous to this parcel of land.
To further complement this design, retail shops are located at street and mezzanine levels within the arcade, ultimately becoming part of the covered connector system for downtown Cleveland.
The office building has its main access on St. Clair Avenue with a gracious entrance through the retail arcade on East Sixth Street. The hotel entrance is on St. Clair Avenue and offers off-street auto access. Registration and Administration, located at street level, provide easy access for guests to downtown, as well as Convention Center activities. The ball room, meeting rooms, and dining room are located on the parking platform. The "H"-shaped floor plate for the hotel ideally accommodates 44 rooms per floor.
The nature of the program and the character of the design provides a unique opportunity for development of a support facility for the Convention Center in downtown Cleveland.

A view of the tower in the model of the complex. Opposite page, perspective view of the complex as it is incorporated in the surrounding landscape.

An overall view of the general model.

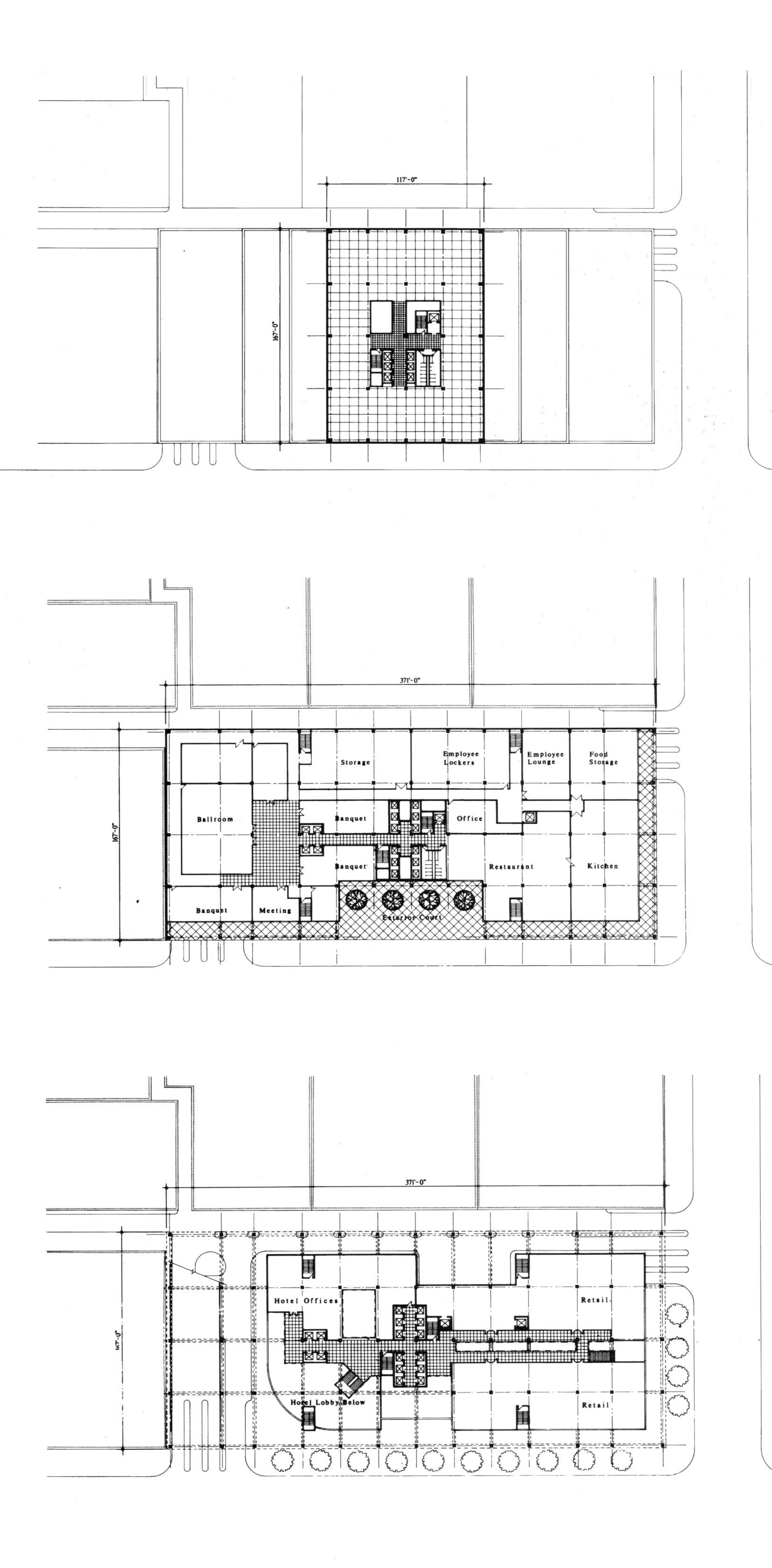

From top of page down, plans of the executive offices (floors 35-39), meeting room, and mezzanine floor.

CLEVELAND CENTER FOR CONTEMPORARY ART
Cleveland, Ohio
1990

The Sears Roebuck Department Store was vacated during the middle 1970's and purchased by the Cleveland Playhouse for the expansion of their repertory theatre. A neighborhood block which included the two theatres and the Department Store has been transformed into a three-theatre complex designed by Philip Johnson with ancillary facilities such as classrooms, rehearsal rooms, dressing rooms, and a Playhouse Club. This occurred during the last decade. The intent was to provide a performing arts center located in "Midtown" Cleveland, Ohio.

The Cleveland Center for Contemporary Art was previously located in two separate areas of the City - Downtown and University Circle. The Board of Trustees' goal was to relocate in a single facility. This was accomplished by acquiring the second floor retail space of the Department Store of approximately 20,000 sq. ft. As a result, the Board achieved two goals: first, combining all their resources into a single space and secondly, complementing the existing performing visual arts center.

The existing conditions consist of a concrete frame building with typical concrete mushroom-capped columns, 25 x 30 ft. on center. The entire space is 75 ft. wide, and 300 ft. long. The existing wood floor in two-thirds of the building reflects multi-stage construction that occurred during the building boom of the postwar era in the Sears and Roebuck Building.

The existing mechanical-electrical systems were removed. Heating and air-condition equipment was located on the roof and a new electrical distribution system which provided exhibition lighting throughout the center, was created in a storage room.

The entire space has been empty from the time the Cleveland Play House purchased the building and their Board of Trustees were pleased to announce the space was leased to the Cleveland Center for Contemporary Art for 2.00$ per square foot triple net. The problem was to create a gallery for traveling exhibitions while providing an exhibition area for regional and local art, a museum shop, educational center, audio-visual center, and ancillary facilities.

The constraints of the space, such as the proportion of the width to length, ultimately became an asset. A strong professional plan was conceived and reinforced by a 100 ft. long curved glass wall creating a visual corridor to the main gallery, while making the museum shop and local gallery visually accessible. The juxtaposition of the spaces complement the ridged geometrical spacing of the mushroom shaped columns.

The major goal of the program was to create the illusion that space was unlimited for variety of art work to be displayed by using a stringent demolition guide and keeping only the essentials, such as the floor, exterior wall and concrete ceiling. The concept that is implement is a painted, red steel frame supporting a glass curved wall that allows the public to view the activity throughout the gallery.

There were a number of alternatives. Building a new building, acquiring an existing building, creating a rigid collection of boxes where art could be displayed within a fixed geometrical form, both new or old, where the circulation might be at random and the display wall was the only priority. The client vetoed the new building and rejected the traditional organization of space, in lieu of a more fluid, spatial design.

Partial view of the main exhibition gallery. Below, second floor plan showing the various functions.

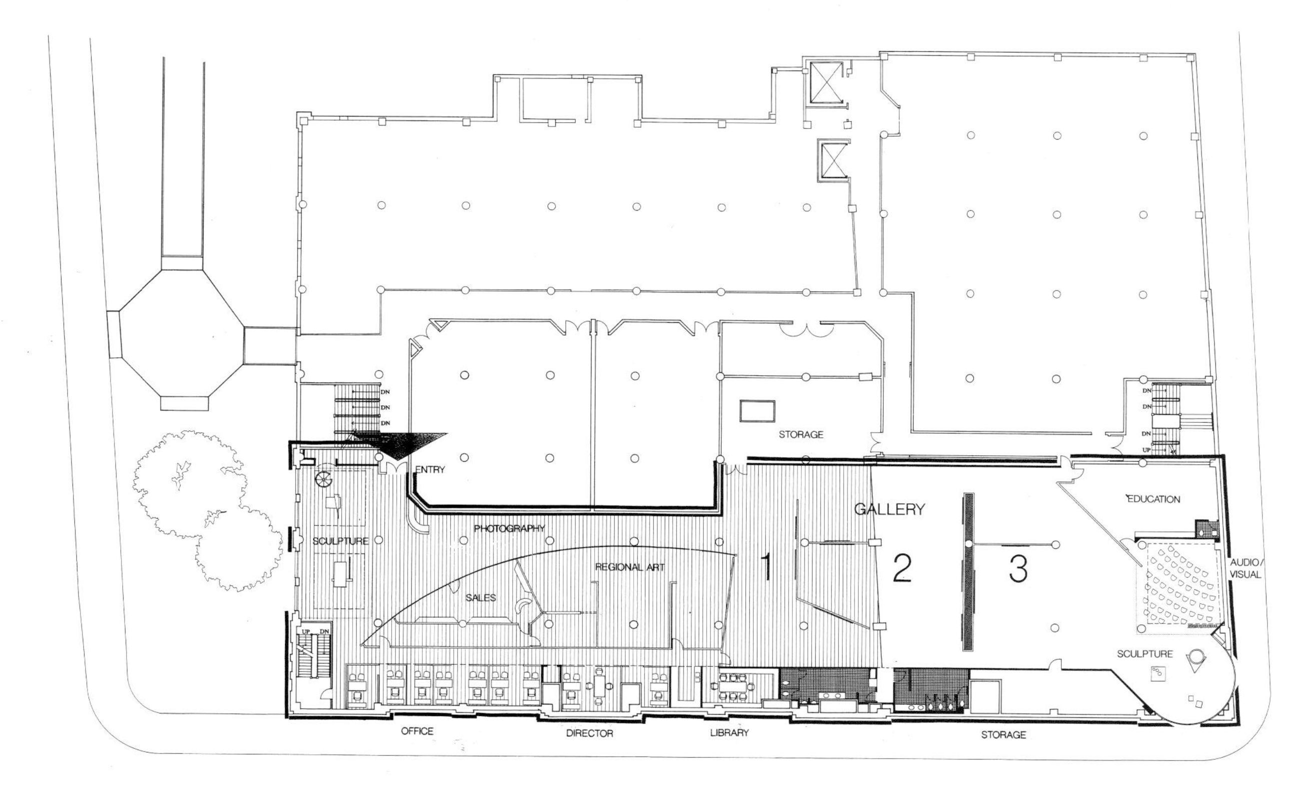

Another view of the Center's interior layout.

The arrangement of functional space is determined by the open layout of the dividing structures.

ASHTABULA HIGH SCHOOL
Ashtabula, Ohio
1991

This planned facility, spatially defined by an innovative program, is both the micro and macrocosm of the entire community. Its primary focus is expanding the networking between teacher and student, teacher and teacher, and student and student.
From the very beginning of the participatory planning process, the community school was mandated by the voters. Each volume of space was programmed, organized, and conceptualized as part of the whole. Requirements for secondary education were consistently supplemented to incorporate community educational opportunities. This new adventure brought about a new vocabulary of spaces. Instead of corridors or hallways, this time the building incorporated boulevards or promenades.
The building is square-shaped. Each quadrant of the square houses a segment of the educational program. The quadrant that accommodates the library also includes humanities classrooms, science laboratories, and other support activities. The performing and visual arts quadrant includes the auditorium, music and art classrooms. The physical education quadrant includes the 1,500-seat gymnasium, along with an auxiliary gymnasium, locker rooms, and exercise rooms. The cafeteria is located in a separate quadrant, which accommodates a kitchen, home economics, industrial arts, and service facilities.

Views of the building model.

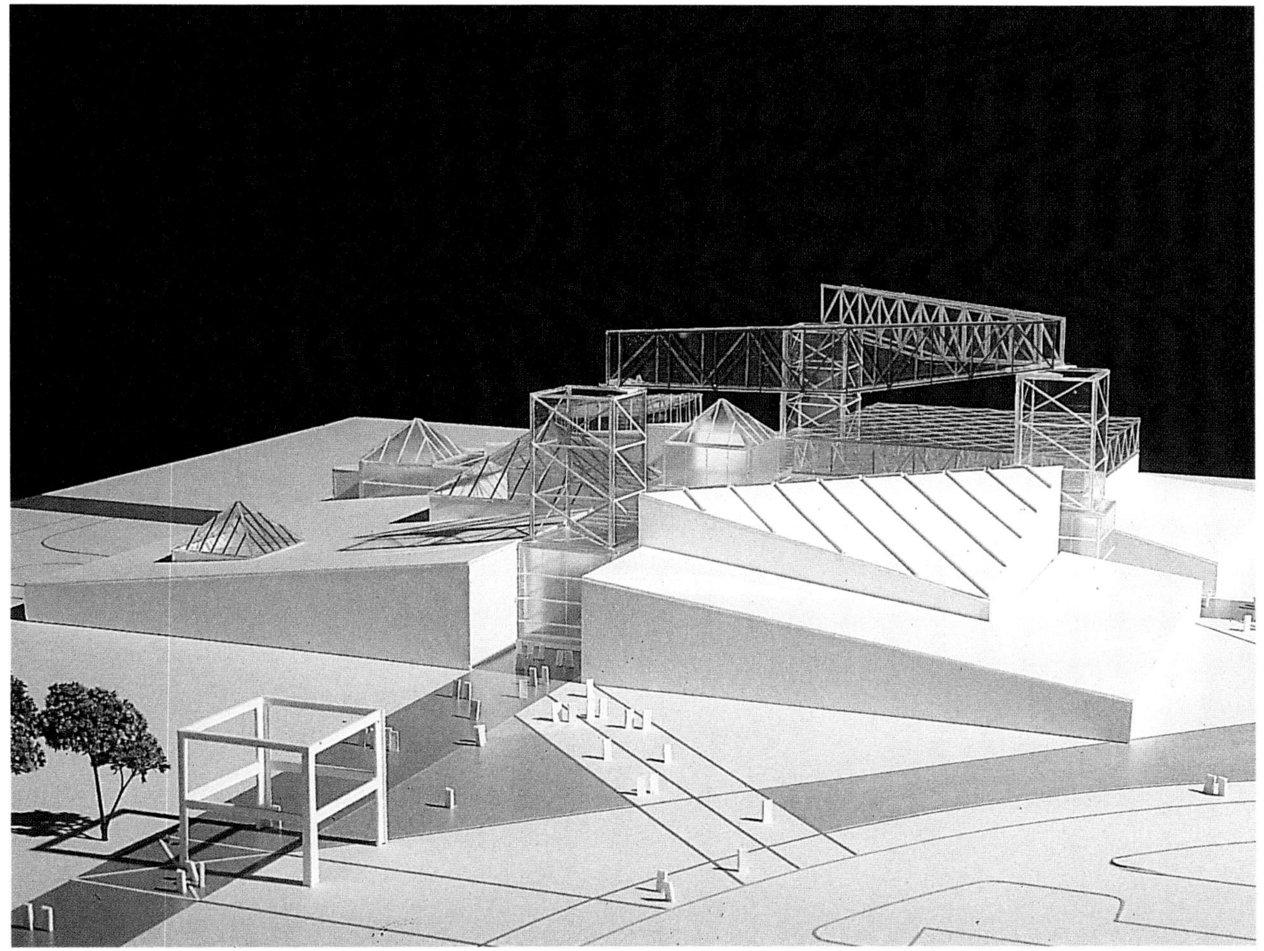

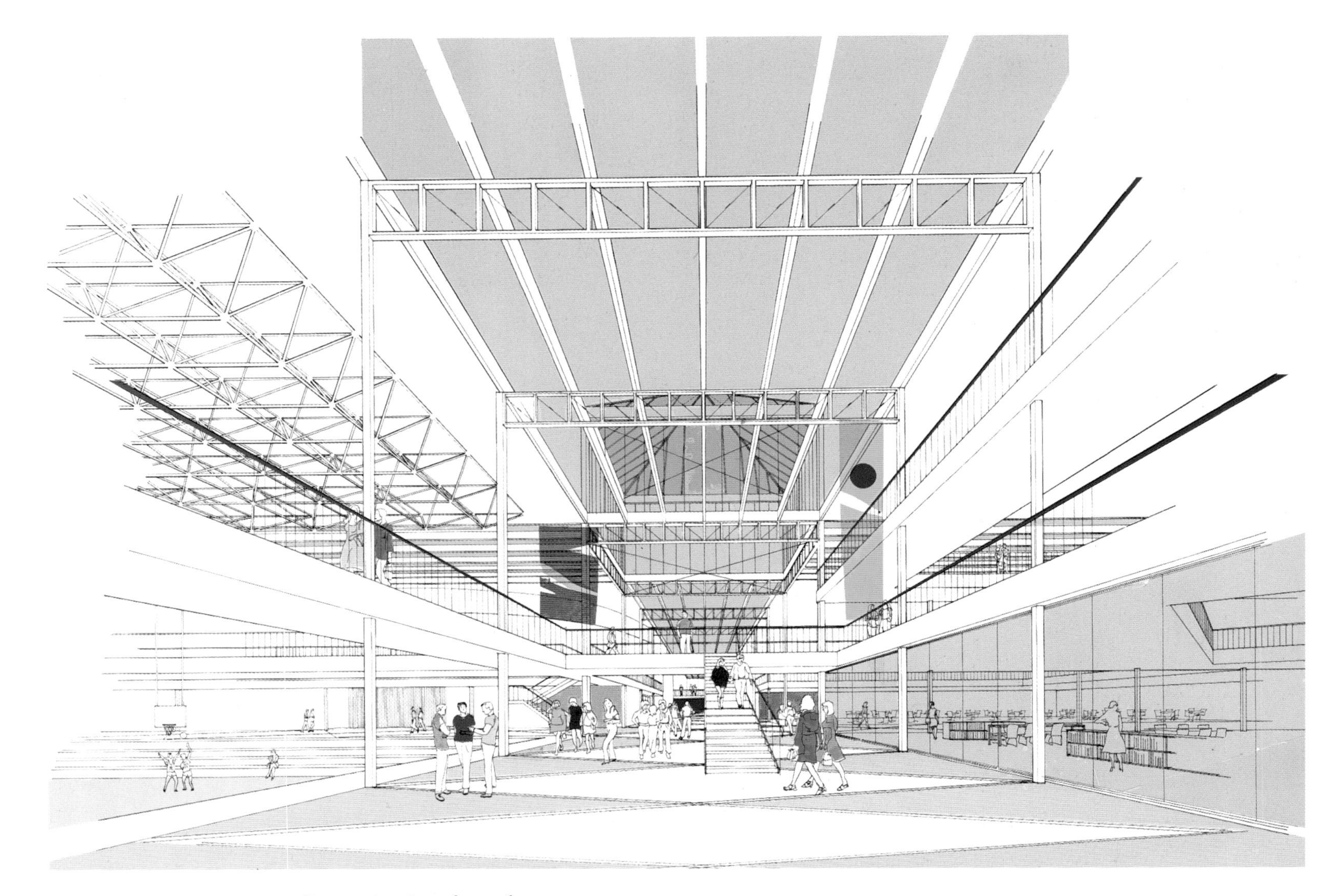

Perspective view of one of the boulevards along which the whole building is organized.

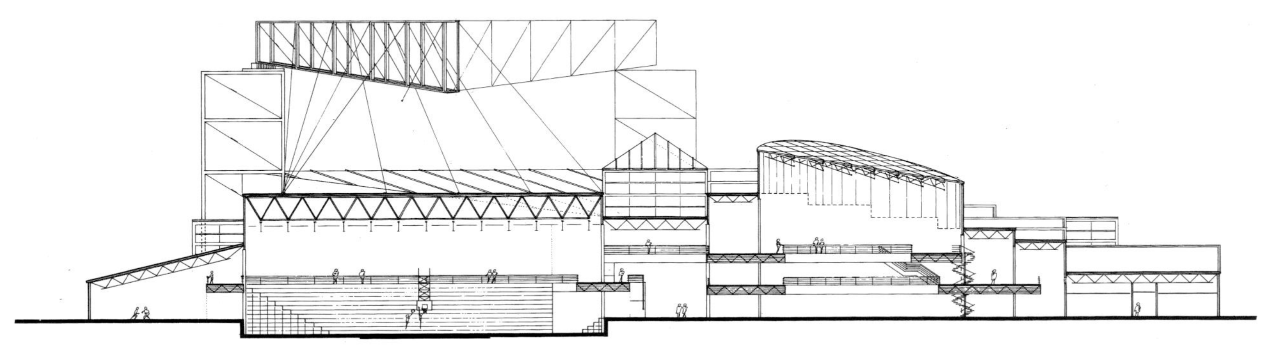

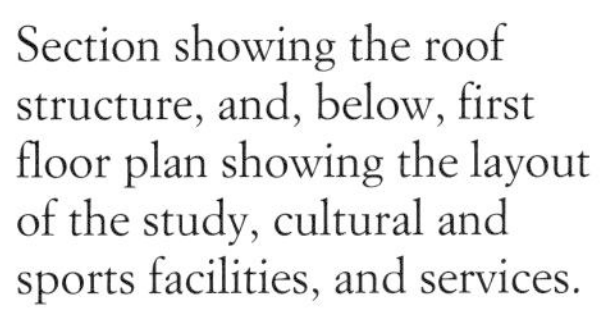

Section showing the roof structure, and, below, first floor plan showing the layout of the study, cultural and sports facilities, and services.

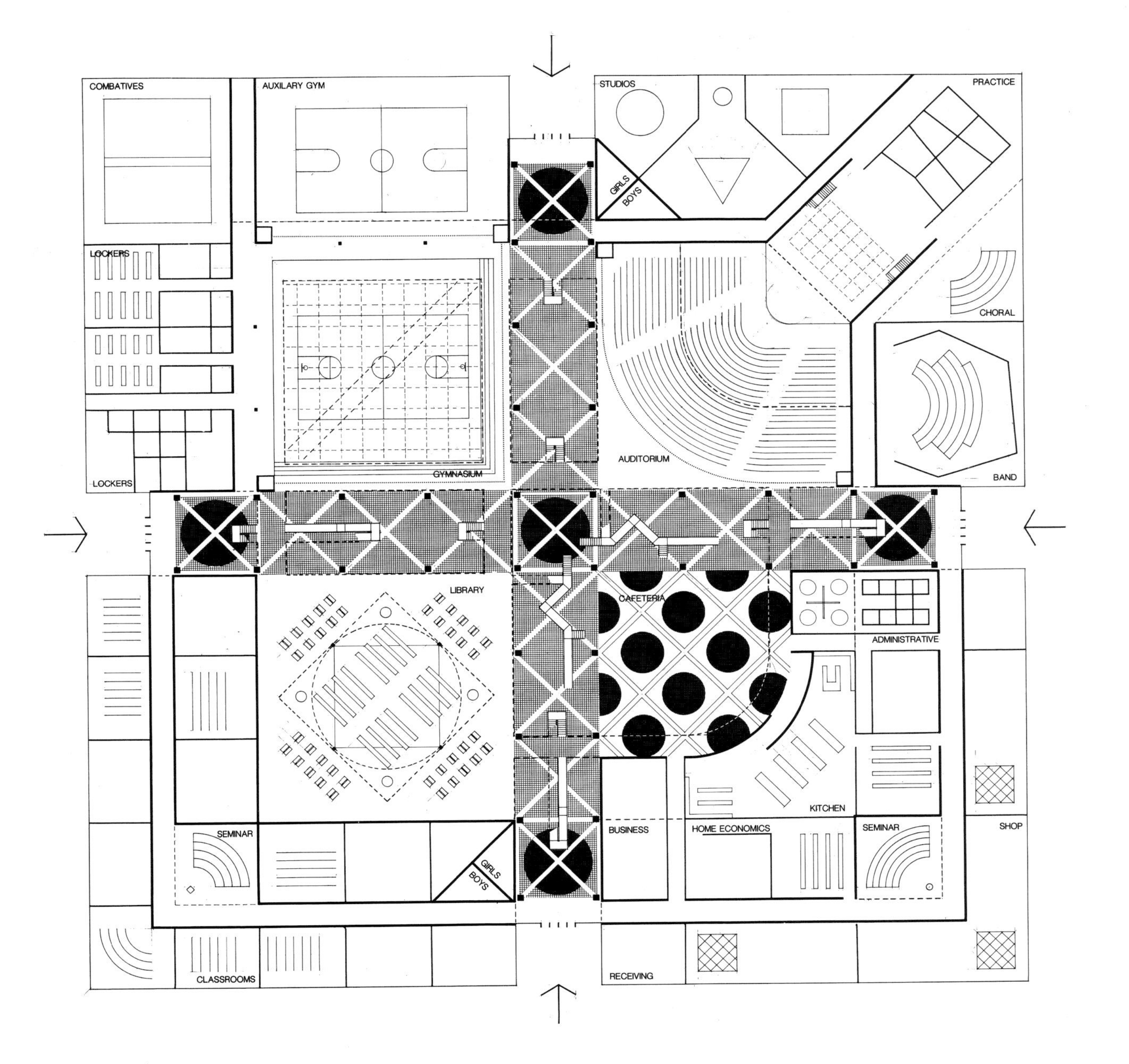

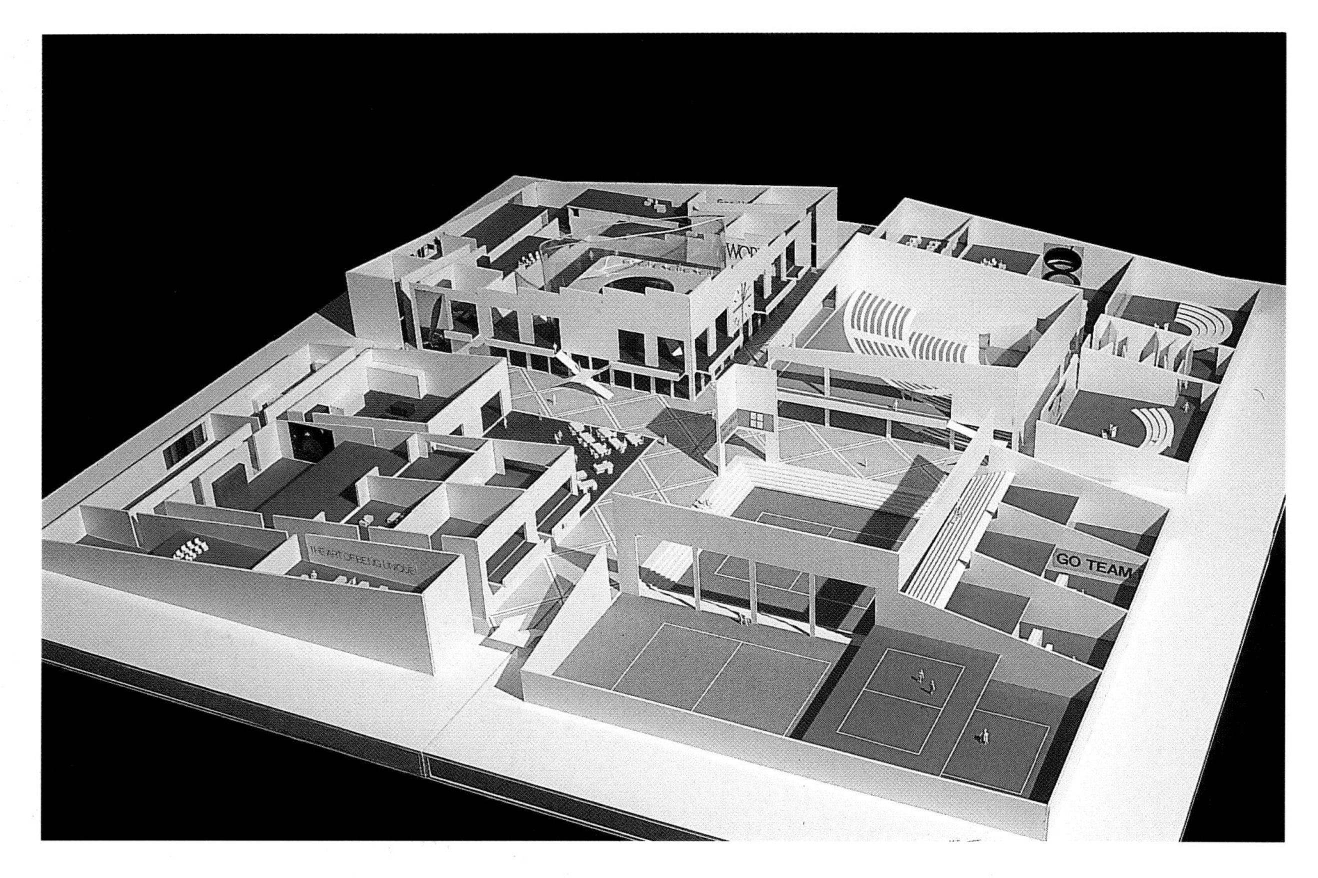

View of the building model.

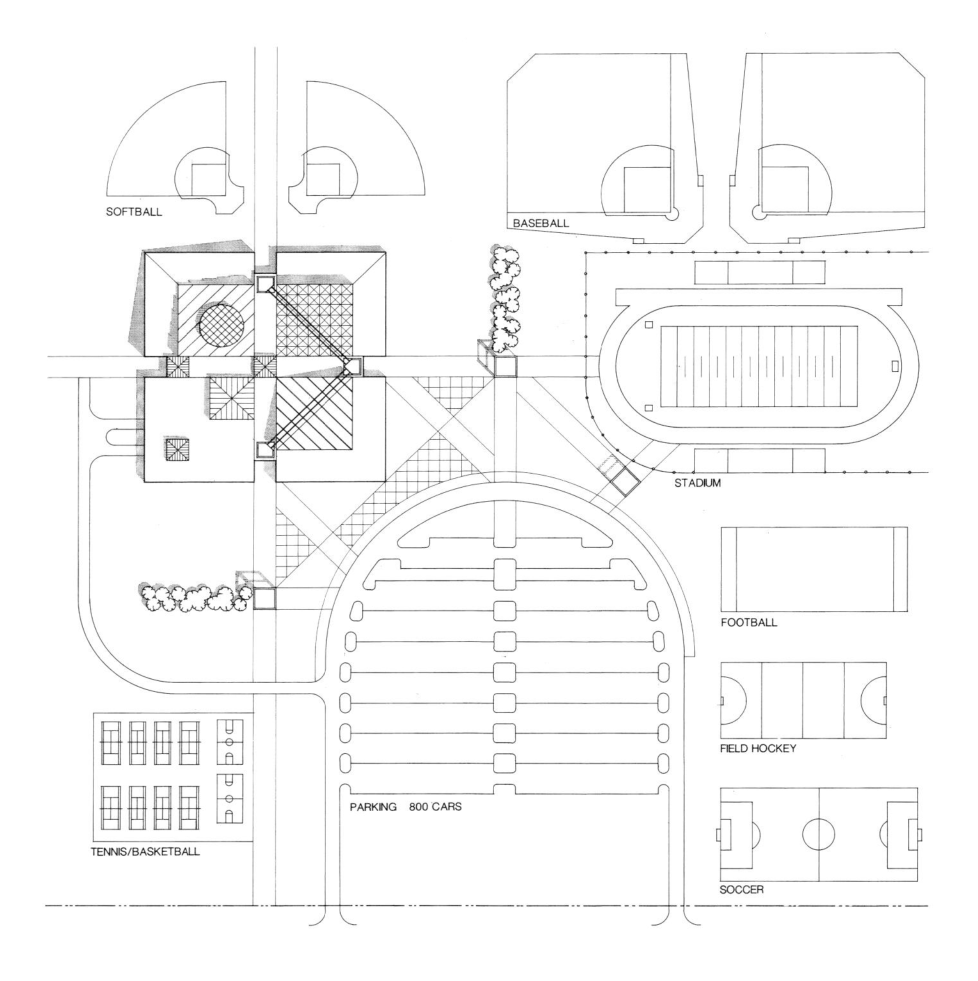

Plans of the outside spaces used for sports purposes.

Aerial view of the model showing the differents coverings of the four sections.

POLYMER SCIENCE BUILDING
UNIVERSITY OF AKRON
Akron, Ohio
1991

The Polymer Science Building is designed to house the University of Akron's world-famous Polymer Institute. It is prominently located on the major east-west corridor of the campus and adjacent to the Auburn Science Center.
The building complex is designed to accommodate forty research laboratories for graduate and doctoral candidates. It is unique in that each lab is designed to provide a maximum of four research stations, with individual offices for each researcher. The design concept allows each laboratory to be located at the corner of the structure, with all services including elevator and stairs concentrated in the center.
The client requested a collegial environment for smaller groups of students headed by four faculty members. This program requirement initiated a collection of vertical atriums creating lab clusters made up of three floors. A typical lab cluster consists of sixteen labs, four faculty members, two secretaries and between twenty-four and thirty students. Each cluster has its own diagonally-located atrium providing continuity between each tower. The lower three floors provide lobby, lecture and display spaces, administration, classrooms, teaching laboratory, and support facilities.
The graduate and doctoral candidates are encouraged to pursue the investigation and discovery of new technology. The transparent shell is conducive to expressing the different functions that are taking place. The building embodies the creative activity it accommodates.

Exterior view of the Polymer Science Building seen from Grant Street. Opposite page, overall site plan.

Transversal section and, below, first floor plan. Opposite page, main facade of the building.

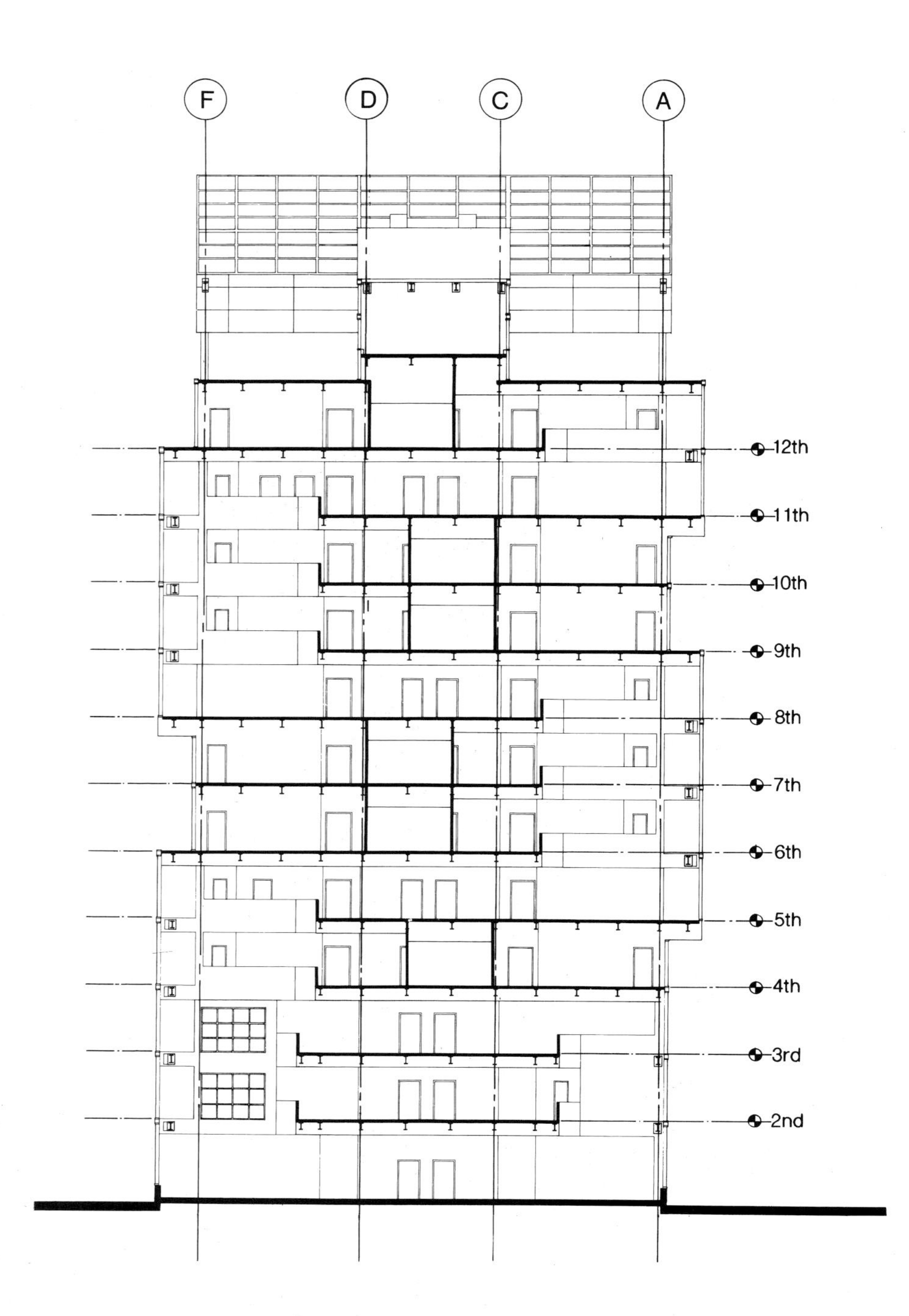

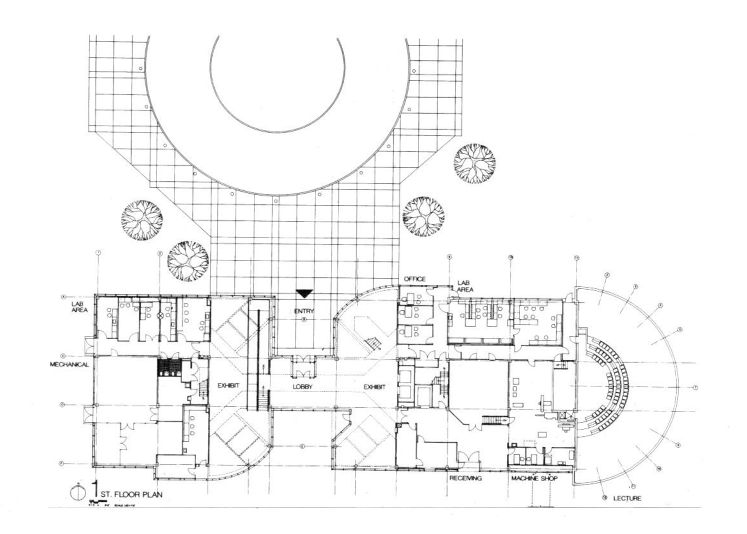

STOP

HUMAN SERVICES AND SUPPORT AGENCIES BUILDING
COUNTY OF CUYAHOGA
Cleveland, Ohio
1992

Richard Fleischman Architects was responsible for all the programming, space planning, architectural and engineering design, interior design and graphics for the six-story, 300,000-square-foot office building in downtown Cleveland which accommodates two county agencies.
The 40,000-square-foot floor plate is a unique design incorporating three multi-story atriums that are organized to help identify and complement the numerous departments and work stations in the building. Reflective and tinted glass panels are used to enclose the fireproof steel frame structure. Space Utilization studies reflecting program analysis provided floor arrangements that create maximum flexibility and efficient operation of the building.
The division of Human Services and its multitude of departments is organized on the top four floors, while the support agencies division is located on the ground floor and lower level. Each division is autonomous and required separate, identifiable entrances, a crucial design component. The design process is a reflection of key department heads who help identify program requirements and draw up space organization charts. Department clusters and individual work stations were analyzed so that ideal solutions could be achieved within the budget.
The building is located in a very important area in downtown Cleveland currently undergoing major urban renewal. It is the first of numerous buildings that are planned for this area of Superior Avenue.

View of the entrance to the Support Agency.

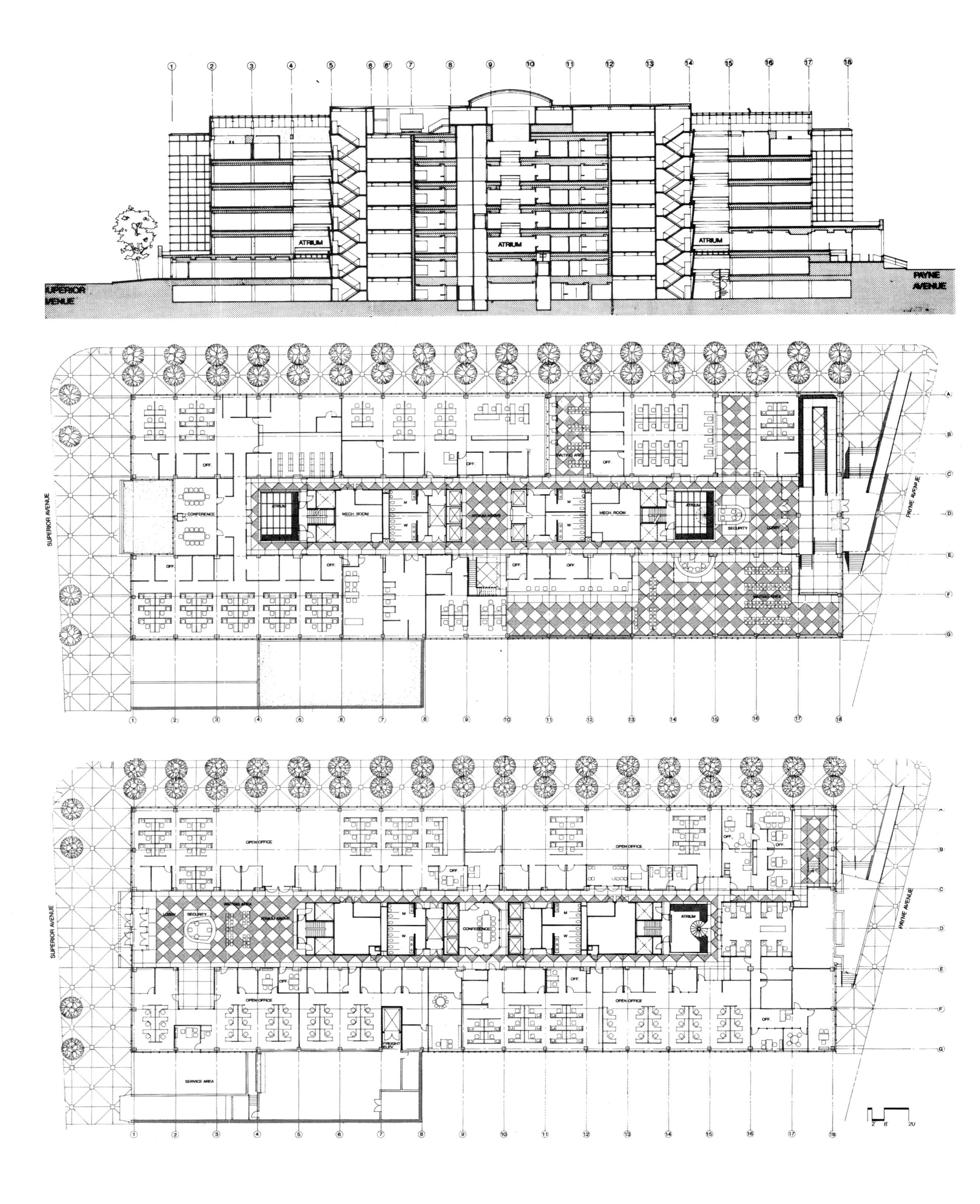
ATRIUM
ATRIUM
ATRIUM
SUPERIOR AVENUE
PAYNE AVENUE
CONFERENCE
OFF.
MECH. ROOM
SECURITY
LOBBY
WAITING AREA
OPEN OFFICE
SERVICE AREA
FREIGHT ELEV.

Partial view of the top-floor canteen. Opposite page, from top of page down, cross section, first floor plan and ground floor plan.

NORTH POINT
INN

BREEZY BLUFF ESTATES
Bratenahl, Ohio
1993

Breezy Bluff Estates, a distinctive residential community located over seven acres along Lake Erie, north of Cleveland in Bratenahl, was once the home of Cleveland's captains of industry. The property is anchored around a mansion joined by two recently-completed and quite startling homes.

Their design is modern: three-story structures with pitched glass and tile roofs; floor-to-ceiling glass in abundance; arched windows. Constructed of steel, glass and cement finish, the development has quickly attracted the attention of the city's leaders-people who will help shape Cleveland in the 21st century. These are futuristic buildings with the same timeless quality as their old counterparts, the majestic mansions of the 19th century. These new homes go beyond state-of-the-art deep into the next century. Their unique design appeals to the dynamic, creative people who will play major roles in the coming decades.

The surrounding mansions, built more than 100 years ago, were progressively eclectic in their day, when their European grandeur helped create a new lifestyle for Cleveland's cultural and political leaders.

A master plan calling for eleven new villas and town-homes on the site was planned from the beginning. The oblong site is zoned for up to twenty-four units, but the strategy was to build just eleven. As a result, each residence offers privacy and an unobstructed view of the lake. The homes are arranged in a half-circle arena, each stepped down five feet, with the lake serving as the "stage." Two of the new homes have been completed and sold to prominent arts patrons.

The first new home on the site was completed in October 1992. Owned by a prominent surgeon, the 6,000-square-foot villa lies near a 50-foot-high bluff overlooking the lake.

Though the concrete slabs and structural steel girders were put in place simultaneously in early 1992 for both new homes, the second, a 3,000-square-foot sister to the first villa, won't be ready for occupancy until April 1993. This second home was purchased by a management consultant who is actively involved in the local art community.

Serving as a unifying architectural base, each residence is constructed on a steel scaffold measuring 40-feet-by-32-feet. Apart from this essential template, Fleischman helps homeowners plan their home's unique exterior and interior spaces, reflecting individual ideas and lifestyles. Homeowners also select personal landscape plans. The master plan, however, calls for a variety of plants and shrubs - with no large specimens to obscure the architecture. A sculpture garden is being designed for the common area shared by homeowners. In addition, a small arena sculpted out of the bluff, expected to host weekend concerts exclusively for Breezy Bluff Estates residents, is planned for the shoreline.

Abundant, spacious rooms open onto each other. Sliding glass doors encourage traffic flow from room-to-room. "The spaces are deceptively simple," said one of the homeowners. "There is great beauty in the apparent emptiness."

Each villa is oriented towards the lake, affording expansive views from floor-to-ceiling windows. The lake vista is accentuated by sailboats in the summer. The breezes are abundant, hence the name of the villas.

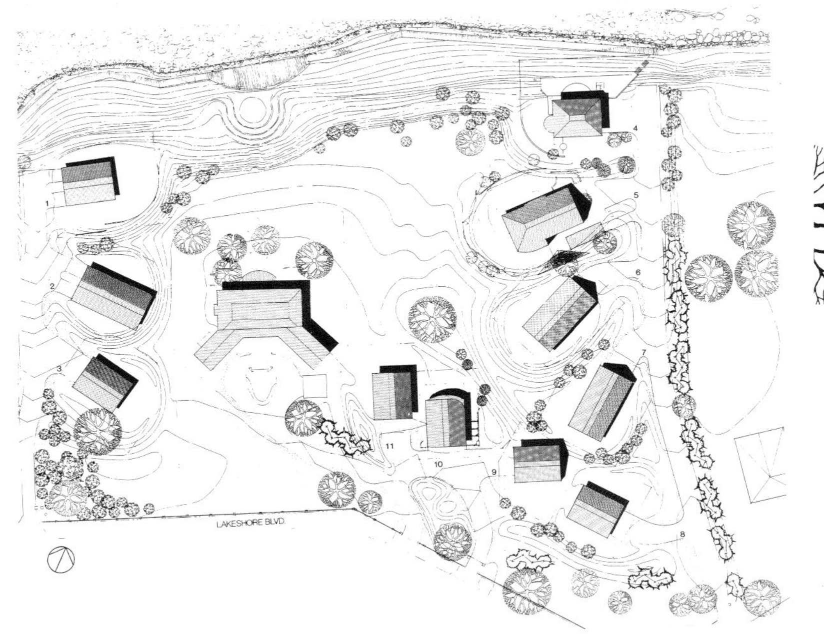

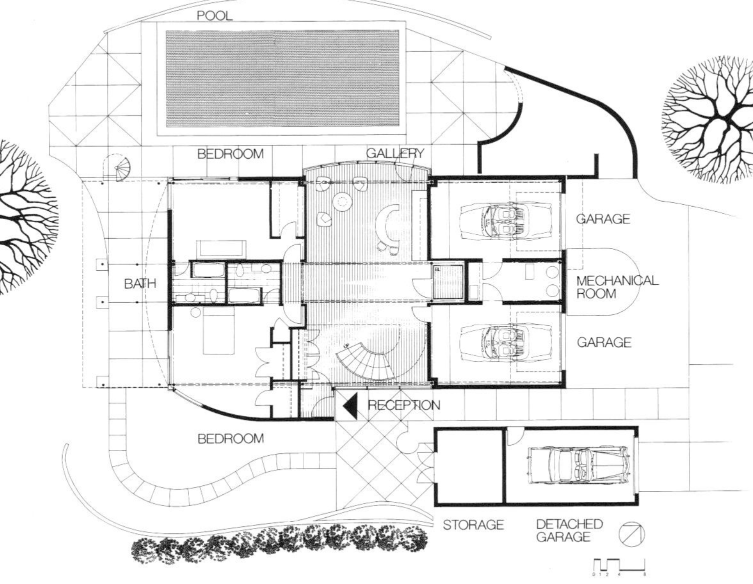

Top of page, view of the lake side of one of the residences. Bottom of page, left, site plan; right, ground floor plan.

The two-level panoramic lounge. The large glass window overlooks the lake and the swimming pool.

Entrance facade of the second completed villa.

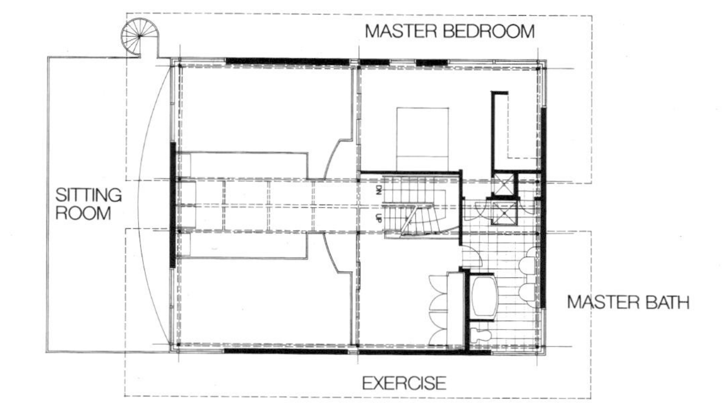

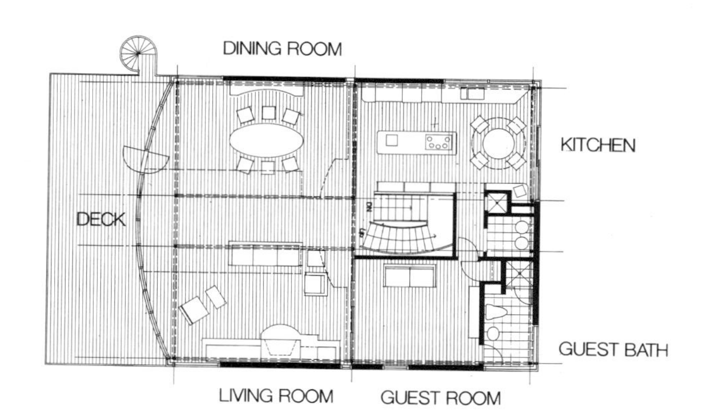

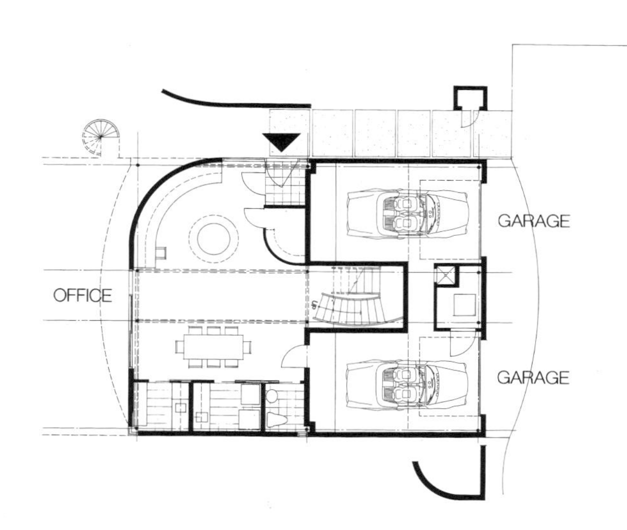

Facade overlooking the lake and plans of the various levels.

The top level of the villa; the skylight allows natural light to permeate the internal spaces.

The master's drawing room seen from the top level.

PLATEAU SENIOR HIGH SCHOOL
LAKE WASHINGTON SCHOOL DISTRICT
Seattle, Washington
1993

A comprehensive high school for 1000 students which separates the Arts and Sciences, Performing Arts and Physical Education into three components connected by a student commons, administration center, and kitchen and ancillary facilities.
The 210,000-square-foot building is organized on a 55-acre site, so as to provide a football stadium built out of earth and additional playing fields for practice, baseball, and soccer.
The two-story Humanities wing is structured so that the second level of the boardwalk is open to the lower level. This open multi-level student boulevard allows access to all classrooms and laboratories. This openness encourages transaction between students and classes during as well as before or after school hours.

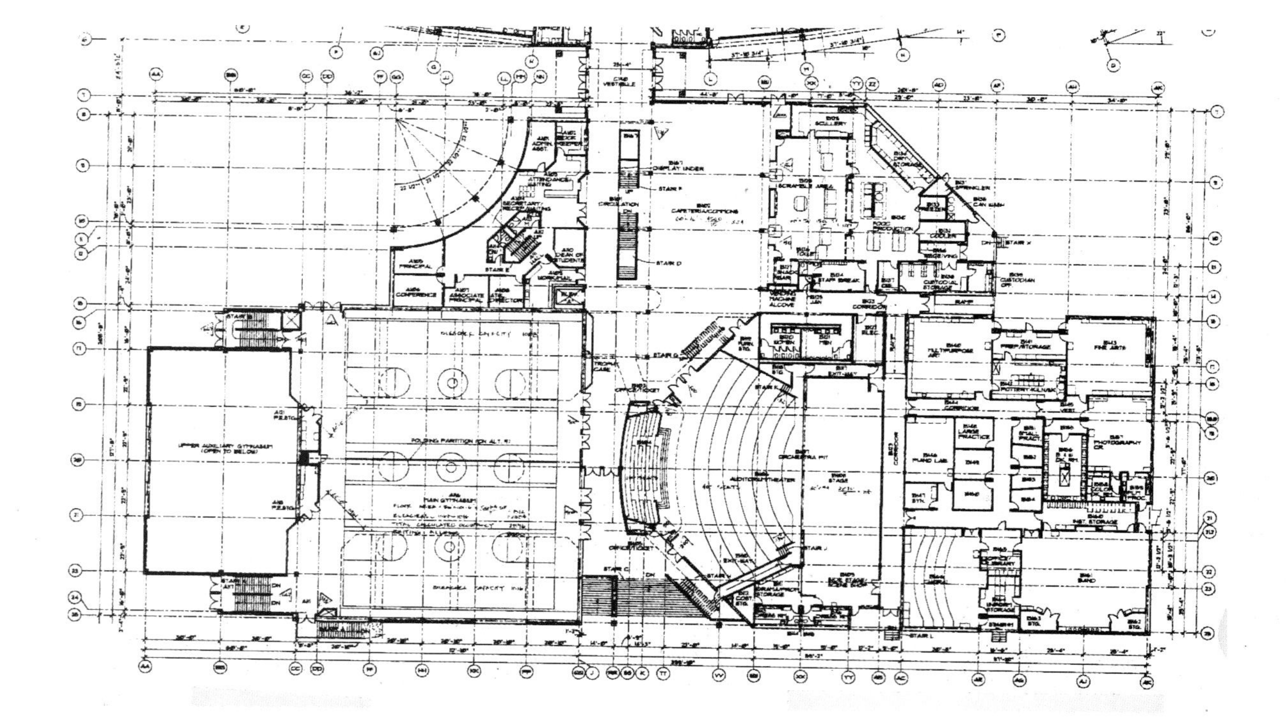

View of the building at the intersection between the two structures; below, a view of the model. Opposite page, plan of the lower level of the building.

View of the gymnasium.

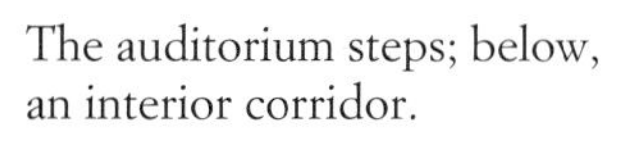

The auditorium steps; below, an interior corridor.

OHIO AEROSPACE INSTITUTE
Brook Park, Ohio
1993

The Ohio Aerospace Institute Building houses a new organization, created by a consortium of several Ohio universities, government agencies, and private companies. The purpose is to facilitate graduate level education in disciplines related to the aerospace industry. By being located next to the NASA/Lewis Research Center, students and faculty will be provided with work and classroom spaces which support their laboratory research work at Lewis.
This dual nature of the Institute is reflected in its design. The public side is entered through a three-story atrium which also serves as a banquet hall for special events. A lecture hall opens off the atrium. The second floor houses classrooms, seminar rooms and a multi-purpose room. The president and the administrative staff are on the third floor. The idea is to provide graduate and doctoral level education and research in disciplines related to the aerospace industry. The Institute wished to create an atmosphere which is collegial and stimulating to both faculty and student. To this end, single or double faculty offices are interspersed with student open office work stations.
The site is located on the south side of the NASA Lewis Research Center. The structure is a steel frame incorporating large spaces which provide flexibility for the various educational programs. Since OAI is a research facility and adjacent to Cleveland Hopkins Airport, sound was an important factor. Special details were incorporated such as roof insulation, insulated glass panels and a unique curtain wall system which minimizes the transmission of sound. Both in its interior spaces, and as an object in the landscape, the building's design is intended to reflect the excitement of the aerospace enterprise. Because of its proximity to the Cleveland Hopkins Airport, its appearance from spacecraft was not appropriate, it is hoped that the forms convey an image consistent with the building's use.

North side of the Institute, with the vertical connections column on three floor levels. Below, site plan. Following pages, exterior view of the building along the south-west side showing the glass structure that physically embodies its ultimate purpose.

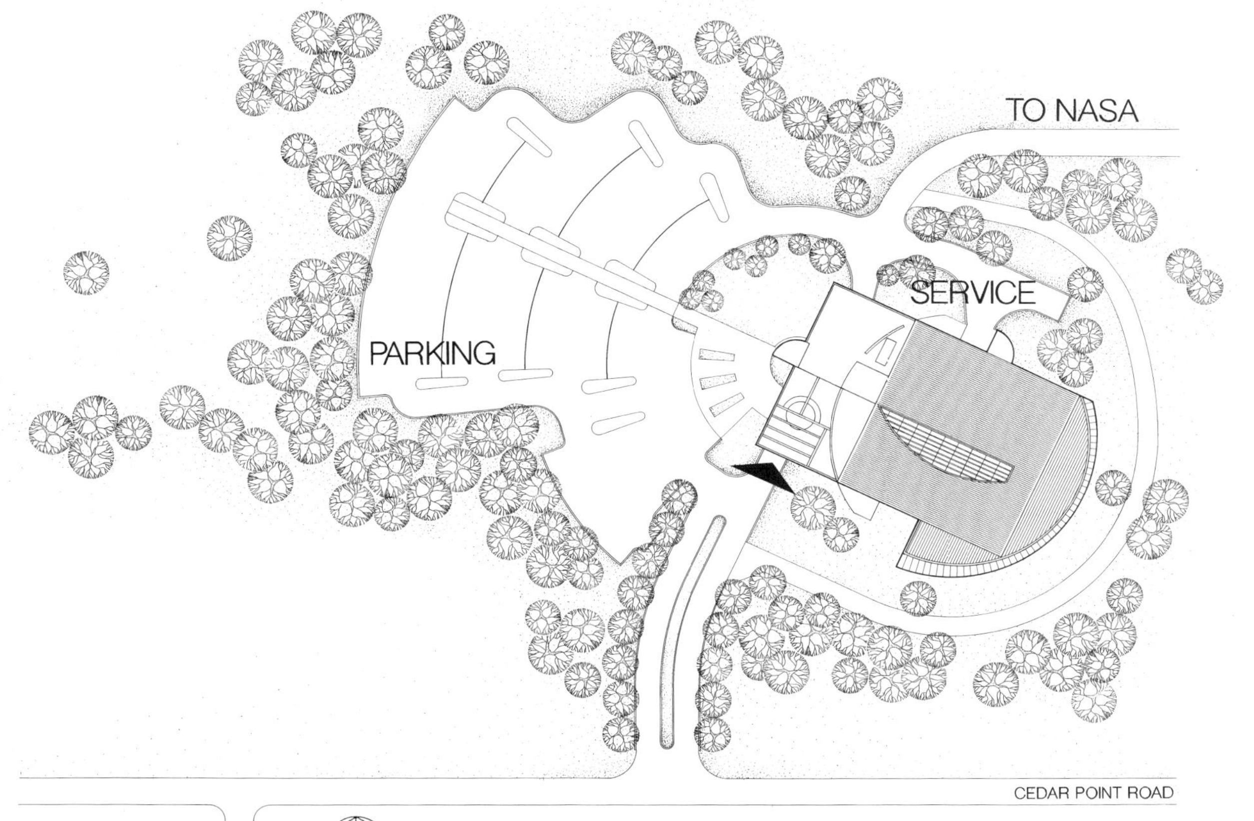

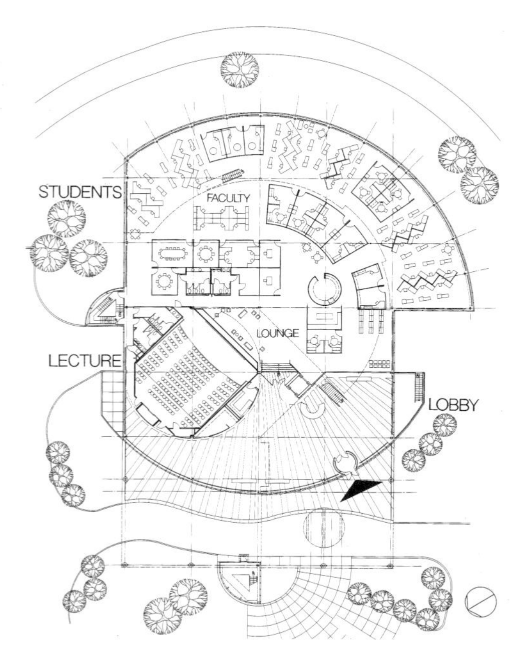
STUDENTS
FACULTY
LOUNGE
LECTURE
LOBBY

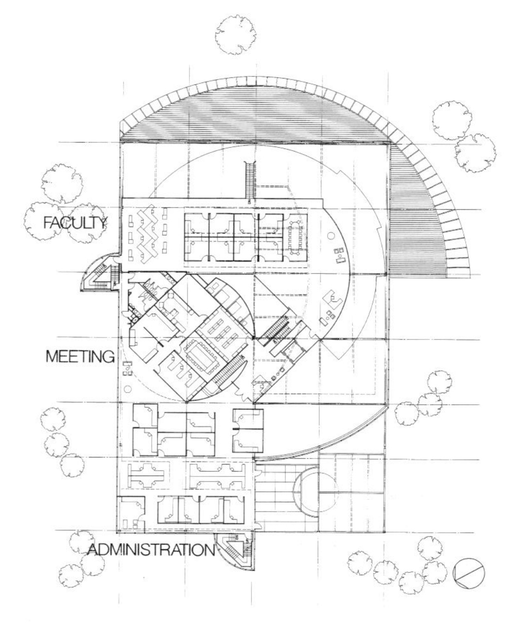
FACULTY
MEETING
ADMINISTRATION

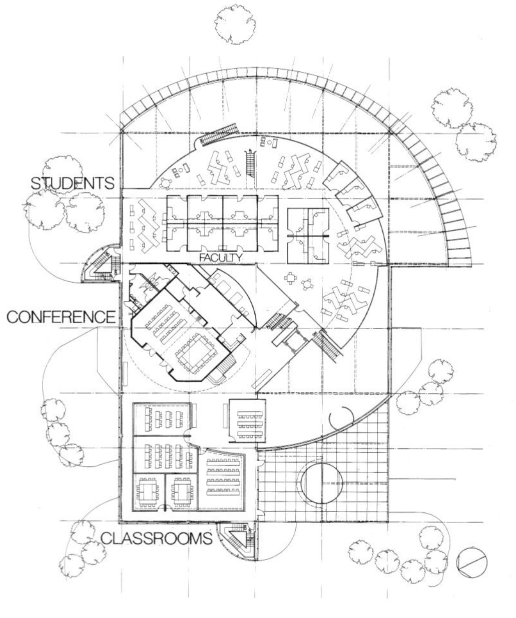
STUDENTS
FACULTY
CONFERENCE
CLASSROOMS

The south façade of the Institute and below, longitudinal section. Opposite page, plans of the three levels of the building.

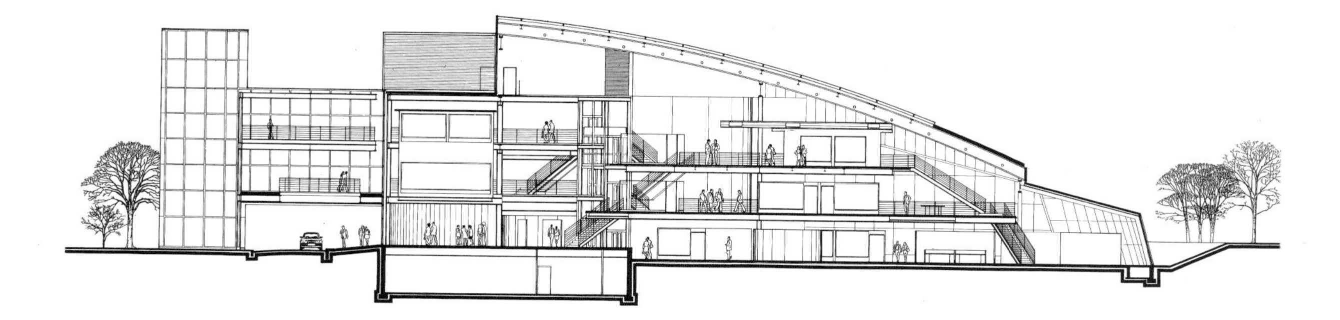

View of the large entrance lobby ovelooked by all of the work areas on the top levels.

View of the top levels.
Below, overall view of the entrance.

CLEVELAND PUBLIC LIBRARY MEMORIAL NOTTINGHAM BRANCH
Cleveland, Ohio
1994

The master plan for the development of Cleveland Public Library provided for the relocation of many of the services that are now accommodated in the main library in downtown Cleveland to a newly acquired facility. The Library purchased the unique 120,000-square-foot Villa Angela building built in 1970, with a view to retrofitting a girl's high school into a public library service facility.
A major program analysis was undertaken for this proposed new facility. It was determined that it was feasible to change the entire high school into a library facility that would accommodate Off-Site Storage (approximately 50,000 sq. ft.) Technical Services (every item accepted by the Library must be catalogued in this location) Library for the Blind and Physically Handicapped (this facility serves Ohio from Columbus north), Training Facility (an auditorium for community activities) Administration and Branch Library (consolidating two existing branch libraries). This is the first time in the U.S. that a major city has organized seven major services on an independent site.
The administration was adamant that the building must change all of its academic characteristics and look like a new library building. Fortunately, the open school plan developed in 1970 for the Ursuline Sisters of Cleveland was designed to accommodate flexible teaching and, therefore, the building could be organized as an open space facility. The gymnasium proved to be an ideal place for three tiers of library shelvings. The existing school's administration offices became the location for Technical Services. The school library now accommodates administration space as well as the training, lecture and computer lab program. A new addition fitted into the structure of the existing building became the new branch library.
Great effort was made to select furniture that reflected the various functions of the building, such as technical services as an office facility and the branch library as a reading and conference space.
Independent entrances had to be organized for specific areas. The branch library must have its own identity independent of the community and staff entrances.

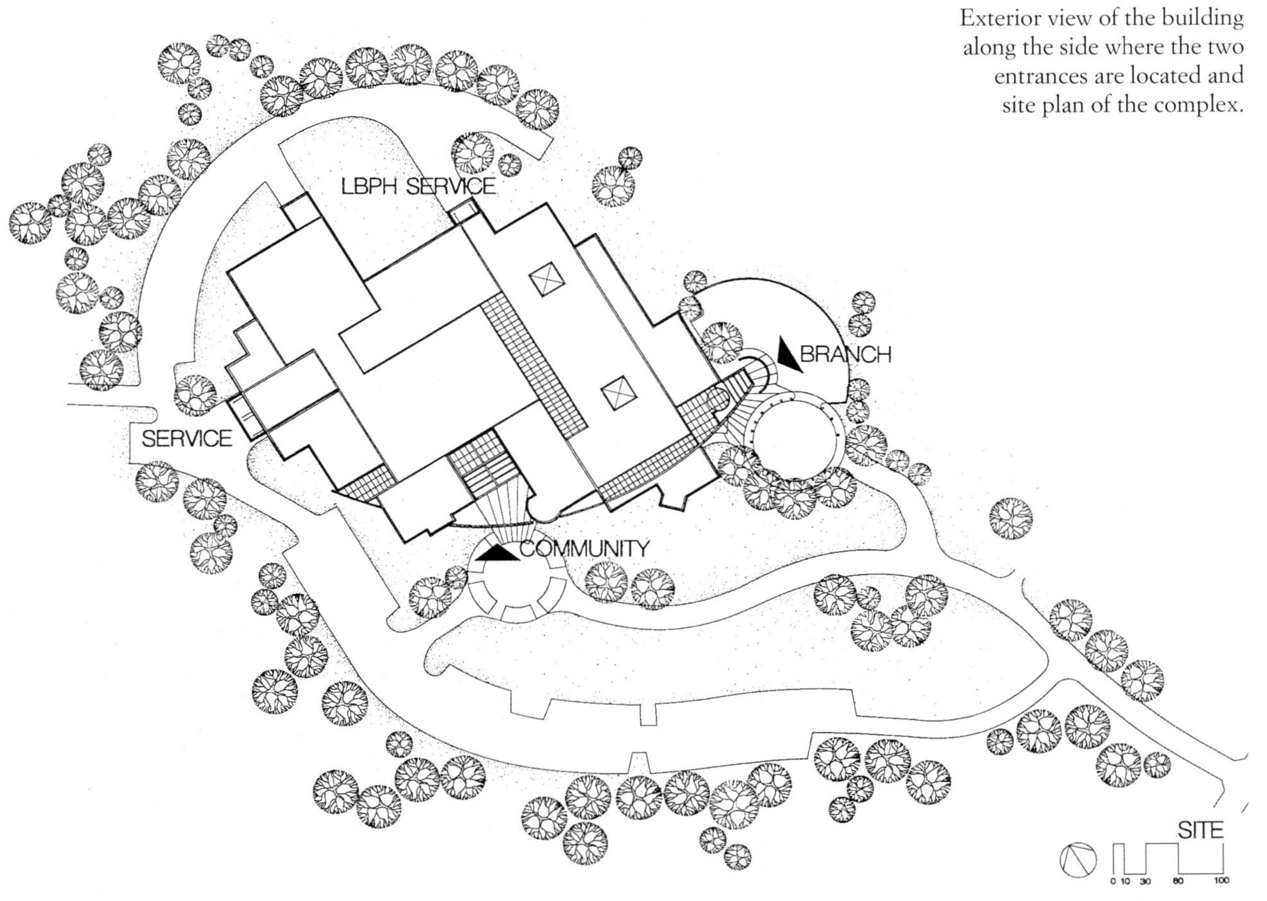

Exterior view of the building along the side where the two entrances are located and site plan of the complex.

Plan of the ground floor of the building and, above, plan of the first floor.

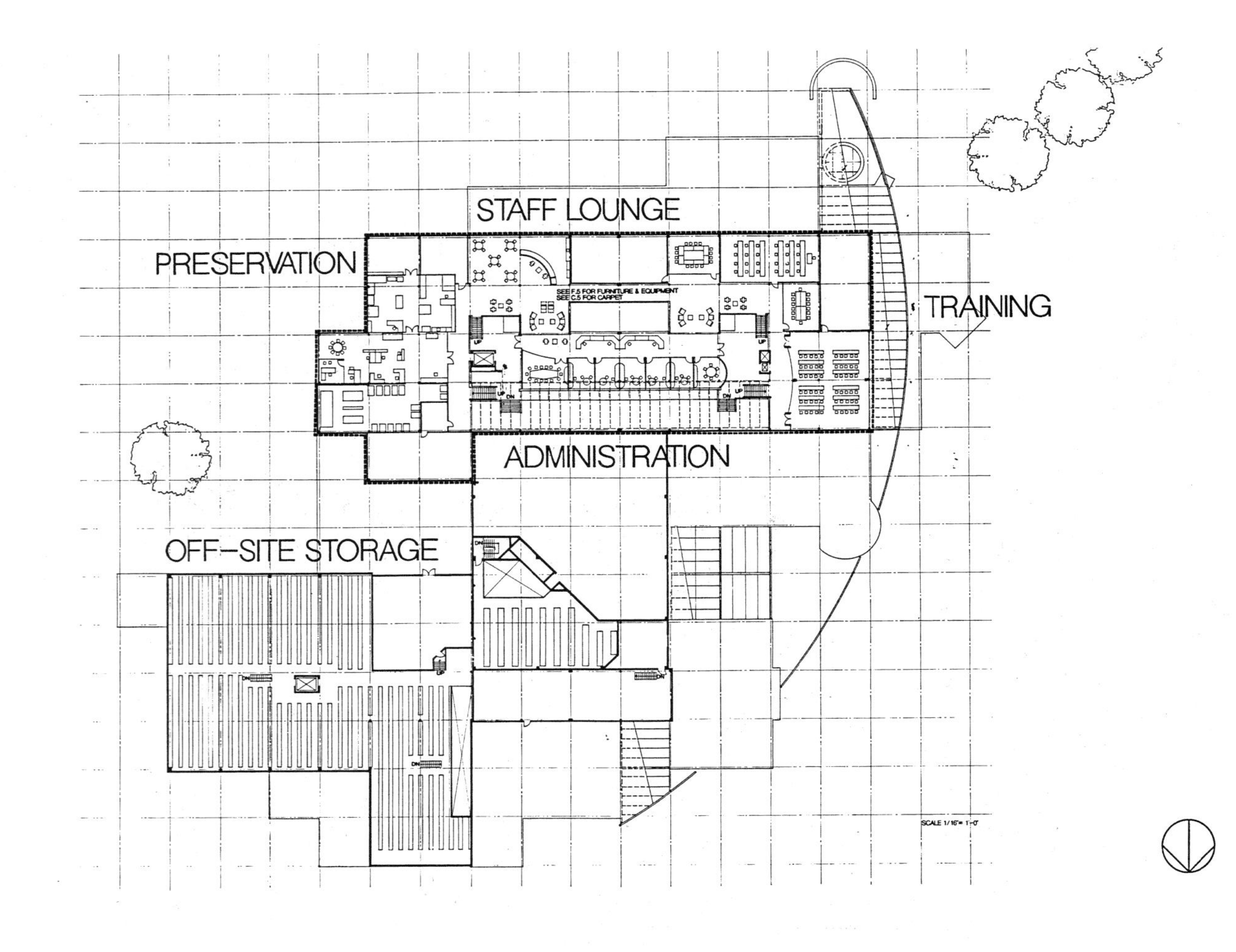

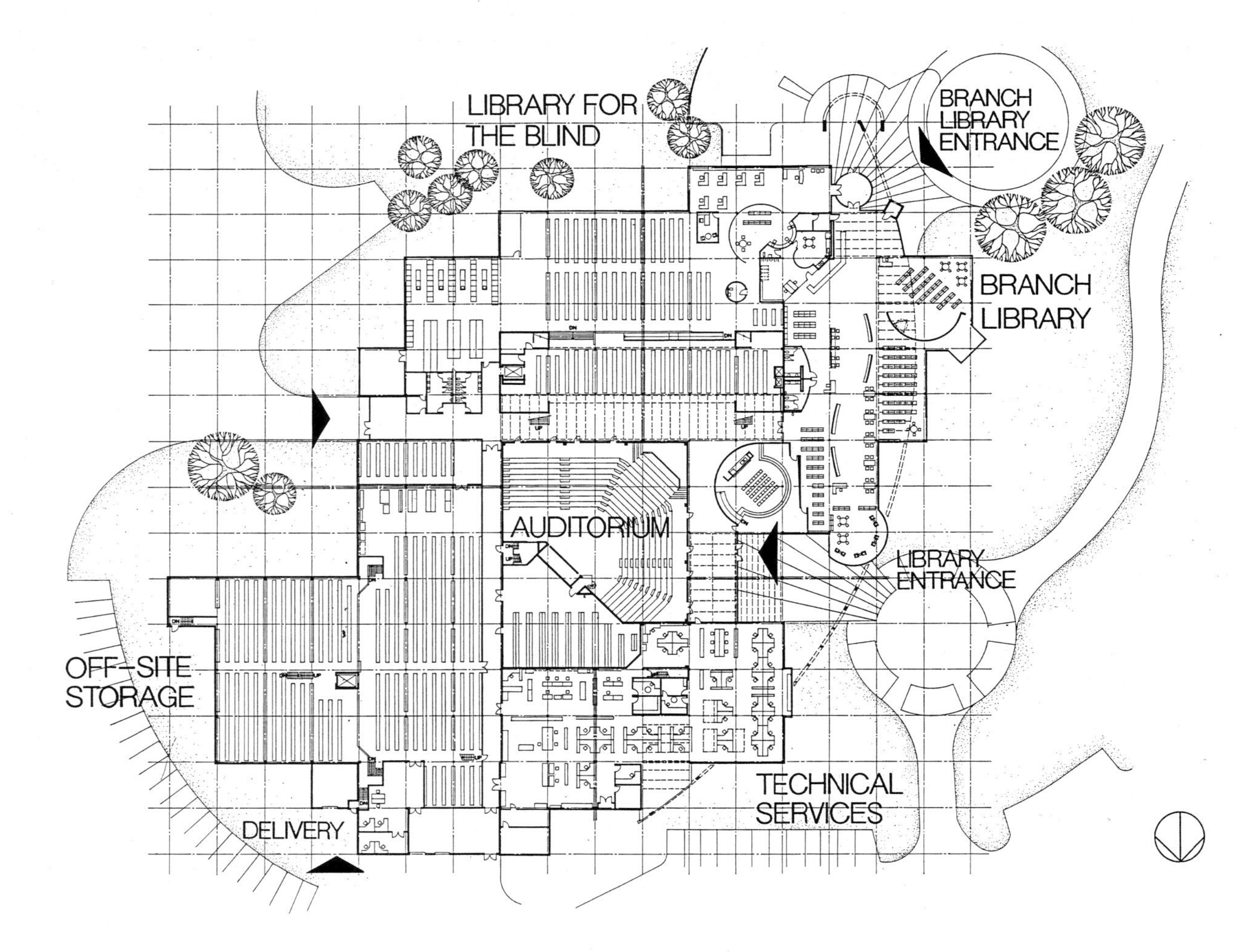

View of the main entrance showing the large sharply overhanging cantilever roof.

View of the library reading room and, bottom of page, view of the auditorium.

The stairway leading to the administration floor beneath the large glass roof.

AUBURN CAREER CENTER
Concord Township, Ohio
1994

Auditorium and Early Childhood Program media and laboratory expansion are innovative new additions to a growing career programs. The auditorium seats 500 and provides opportunities for different seating arrangements for lecture, auditorium and thrust theatre. A.D.A. requirements are fulfilled through upgrading of the existing entrance to allow access for the handicapped, as well as conforming seating and entry accessibility in the new construction.
An Early Childhood Program, a Technical Preparatory Program with physics, biology and computer laboratory spaces, a Library/Media Resources Center and expanded Administrative Offices are also included.
The building incorporates current state-of-the-art tele-communications with facilities for a media retrieval system in all classrooms and assembly spaces, video production and editing facilities linked to each classroom and the auditorium space with potential for linking up with associated schools to disperse and receive additional information.
A two-story commons and reception gallery links the two wings of the new addition. The vaulted skylit main entrance provides an expansive circulation and student meeting area for all the areas of the existing facility, eliminating congestion caused by existing narrow corridors and low ceilings. Both spaces are distinctive features of the building's two principal entrances.

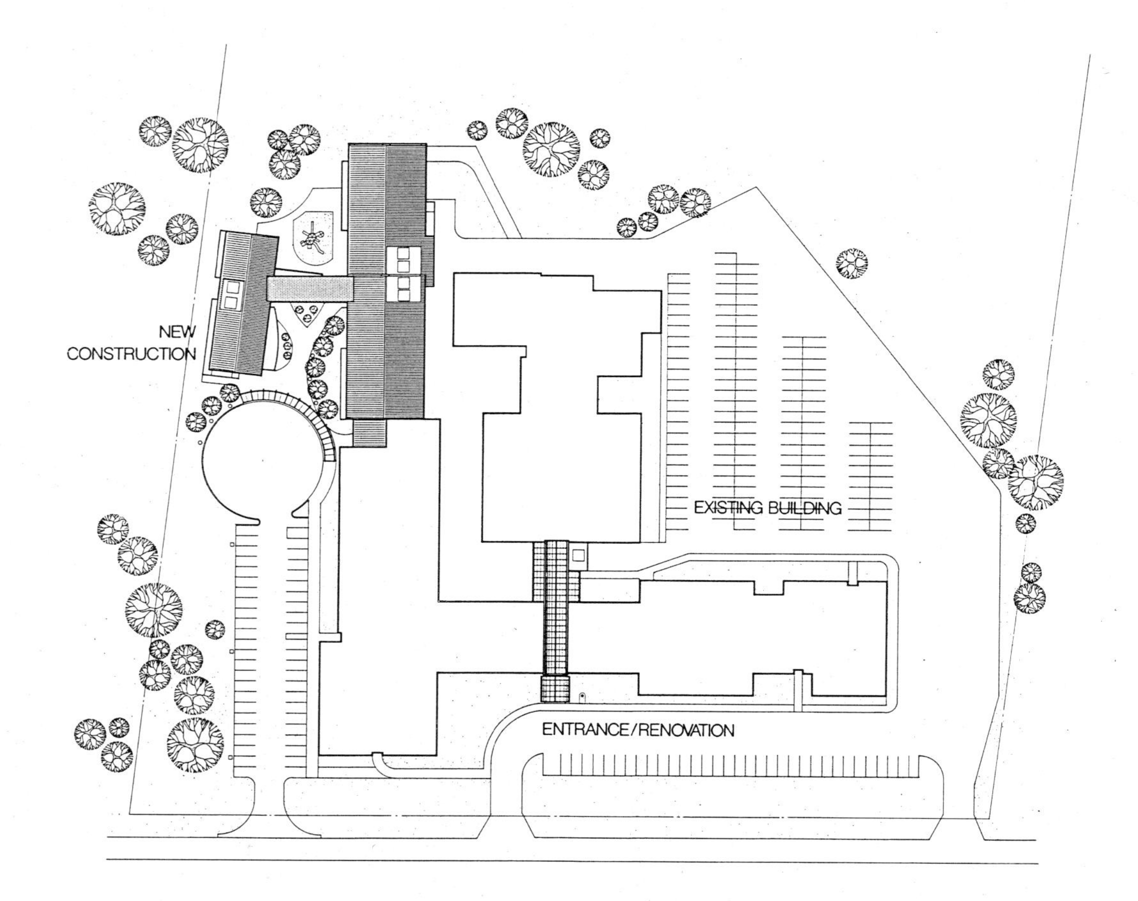

Two exterior views of the new building showing the covered entrance path. Opposite page, site plan showing the new construction.

Plans of the ground floor
and, above, first floor.

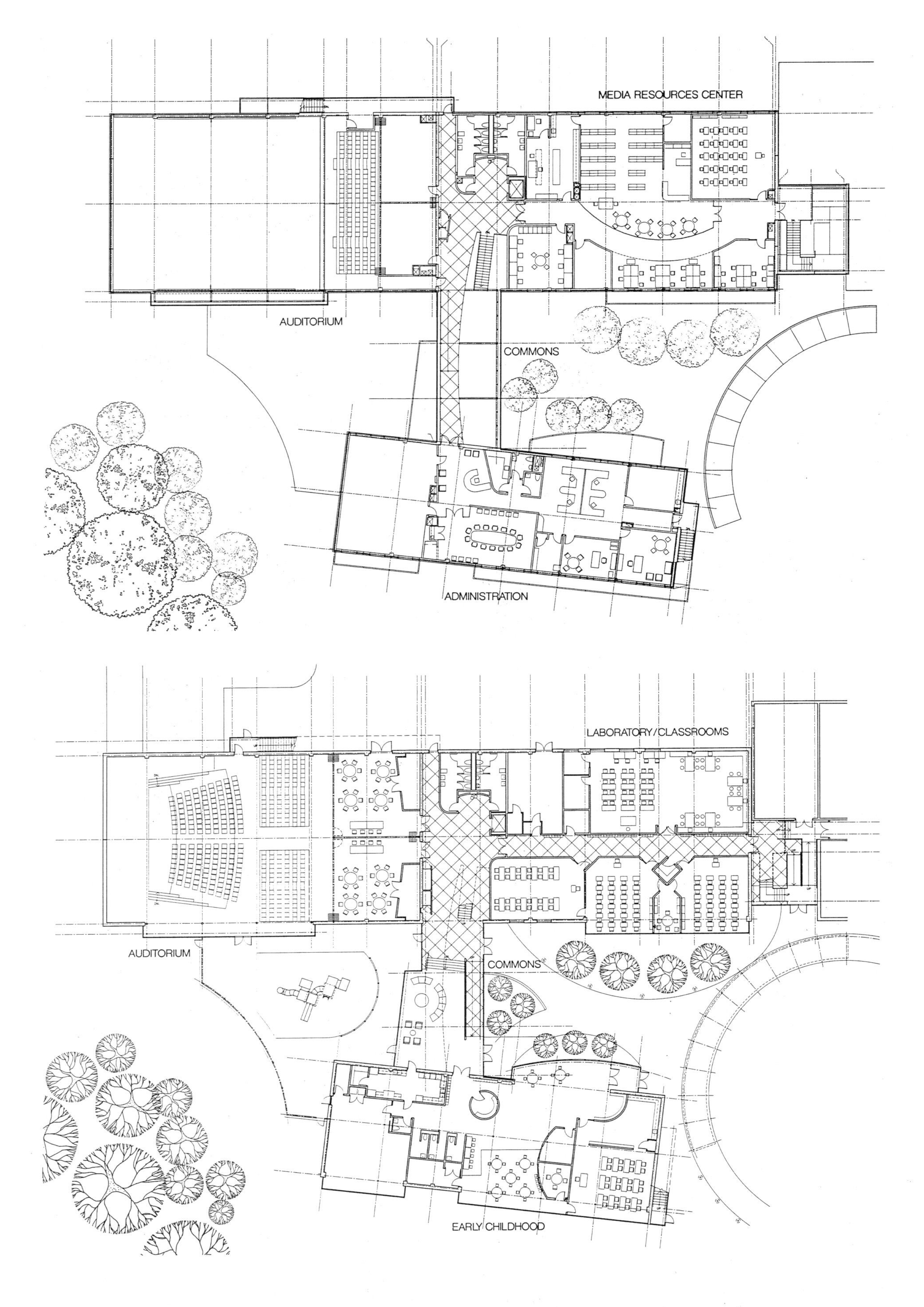

View of the auditorium; bottom of page, an exterior view of the pre-school children's area.

THE ENTERTAINMENT WHEEL
Cleveland, Ohio
1995

Size, image, mobility and illumination are all components in the conceptual creation of a symbol that would attract Clevelanders, visitors, regional and international tourists during the coming decades.

The Entertainment Wheel consists of 24 gondolas. Each gondola is fabricated as a steel truss sheath in two layers of specially designed glass. The dining/observation platform in each cylinder allows for unlimited views of the City of Cleveland and is suspended from the circular structure by means of mechanical gears designed to maintain stability.

The glass gondolas are designed in a manner that permits maximum flexibility for vendors while fostering both psychological and physical security. Each gondola will have a galley for a food and beverage service. A single toilet facility will accommodate the needs of the public. Depending upon each vendor's or caterer's requirements, seating may vary from 18 to 28, and reflect the cuisine and ethnic diversity of the City of Cleveland. The decor will be the responsibility of the vendor and will conform to the design guidelines determined by the development team.

The steel frame of the gondola will consist of 5-inch round steel tubes, 10 foot on center connected by steel tubes that reinforce and shape the cylinder. All the components of the gondola will be constructed within the 20 ft. diameter frame, including dual 9/16-inch plate glass walls separated by a 6-inch air space. Each gondola is attached to the Wheel by a set of mechanical gears that ensure the speed is constant and controlled to allow comfortable ingress and egress.

Public access and service access are located at opposite ends. This allows for maximum visibility along the curved surface. It is proposed that all food preparation should take place in the service podium, very much like a catering service. The Wheel will take one hour to make one complete revolution, allowing adequate time for both the public and service staff to gain access to their selected gondola.

Similar to the technology at Epcott Center, a moving platform adjacent to the gondolas will move at the same acceleration rate as the Wheel allowing easy access to the public. It is estimated that 10 minutes will be sufficient to enter each cylinder before commencing a major cycle.

The podium is approximately 150 feet in diameter and 20 feet in height and will accommodate kitchen and other ancillary services.

The movement of the Wheel is generated by eight jet engines, strategically located within the construction of the frame, allowing consistent and controlled motion. Emergencies may occur and methods are available to accelerate the Wheel to allow egress when required.

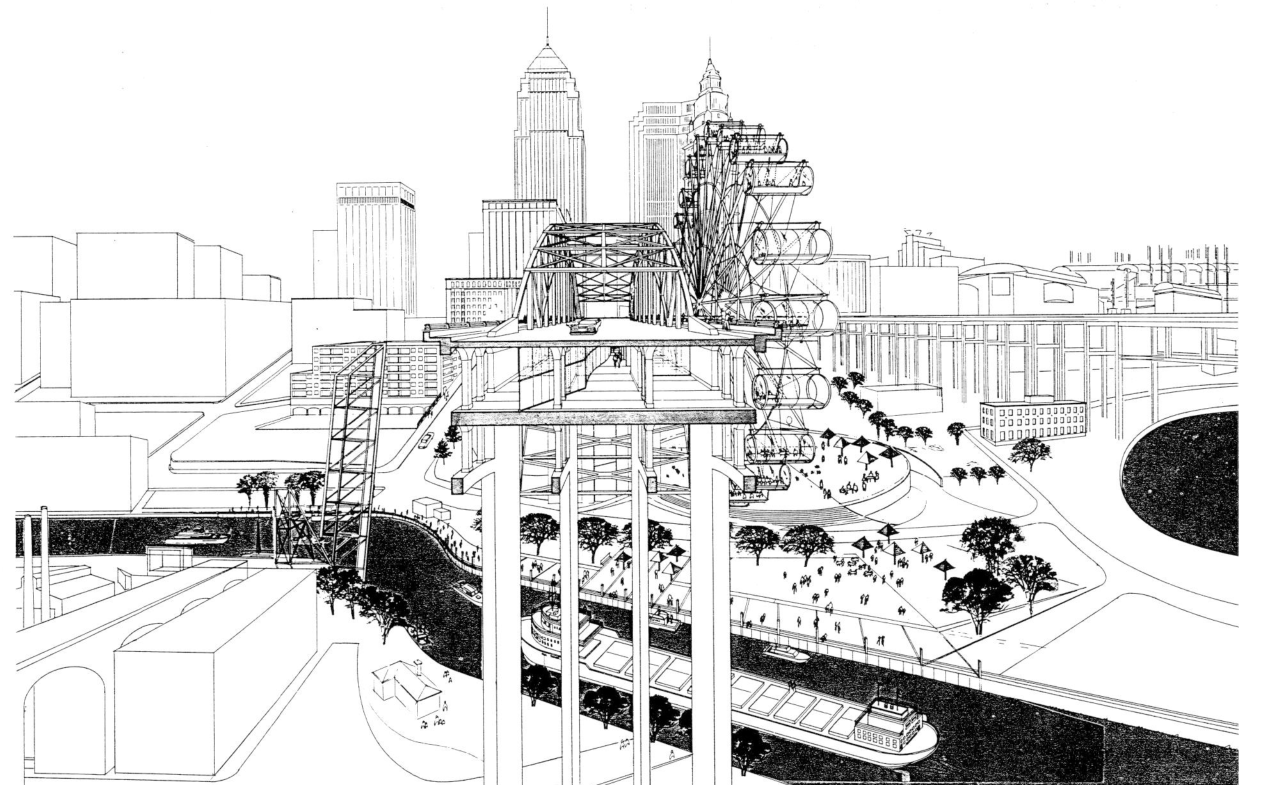

A perspective view of the Entertainment Wheel and, above, a view of the model merged in a possible landscape.

CLEVELAND CONVENTION CENTER
Cleveland, Ohio
1995

The purpose of this planning study is to encourage the City leadership to re-visit the existing site of the Convention Center and to realize that the Mall concept devised by Burnham in 1909 can actually be accomplished. The benefits would be manyfold: expanding the Convention Center to compete in the global marketplace and creating an opportunity to build a variety of other structures such as a federal courthouse, a world trade center or other types of public buildings that would enhance this axial plan. Burnham's plan proposed that a railroad station be positioned at the north end of the Mall as an architectural closure for a classically-designed open space. It is our intent to reflect that planning strategy.

This planning concept would combine an expanded Exhibit Hall, with minimum columns and ideal height, with a transit center and the proposed public building and new Convention Center entrance. This seamless collection of structures would be interconnected by a continuous underground walkway system, tying transit facilities to the Convention Center, hotels and public buildings. This proposal, we believe, would give Cleveland a unique, state-of-the-art facility capable of competing on the international stage and complementing all that is currently being developed in downtown Cleveland, including North Coast Harbor. The goal is to make Cleveland a first class visitor destination.

The proposed expanded Convention facility will cover over 550,000 square feet and extend north beyond the Conrail tracks with a new entrance hall equivalent in size to a Public Square. This new multi-level facility will provide a podium for a proposed multimodal transportation center that will accommodate Amtrak, Waterfront Transit line, interstate bus facilities and an innovative public building such as a world trade center, courthouse, etc. of approximately 550,000 to 900,000 square feet.

The existing fountains and parking garage over the present Exhibition Hall would be removed, together with the 30' x 30' module of concrete columns, and replaced by a far more efficient 100' x 100' column module. The Mall itself would be restored as a public open space with strategically located skylights, providing light and openness to the exhibition space located below. The purpose is not only to expand the convention Center along a north-south axis, but also to allow this area to connect to the multi-level public auditorium on the east side and the new meeting rooms and banquet facilities located in the proposed new hotels to the west.

As the Convention Center will expand north of the railroad tracks, it is recommended that a major public facility be located along this axis. At the present time, a world trade center is being contemplated, as well as a federal building and U.S. courthouse and other facilities such as a hotel or office building. In any case, it is the consensus in the area that a significant building be located at the end of the axis to provide closure for the Mall group as planned by Burnham.

This expanded convention facility will act as a major connector between the center of downtown, Public Square, and the current development at North Coast Harbor, which includes the Rock and Roll Hall of Fame and the Great Lakes Science Museum. Underground walkways acting as a promenade with adjacent retail services will continue from Public Square to North Coast Harbor. This boardwalk type of circulation will also directly connect the proposed new hotels to the expansion space.

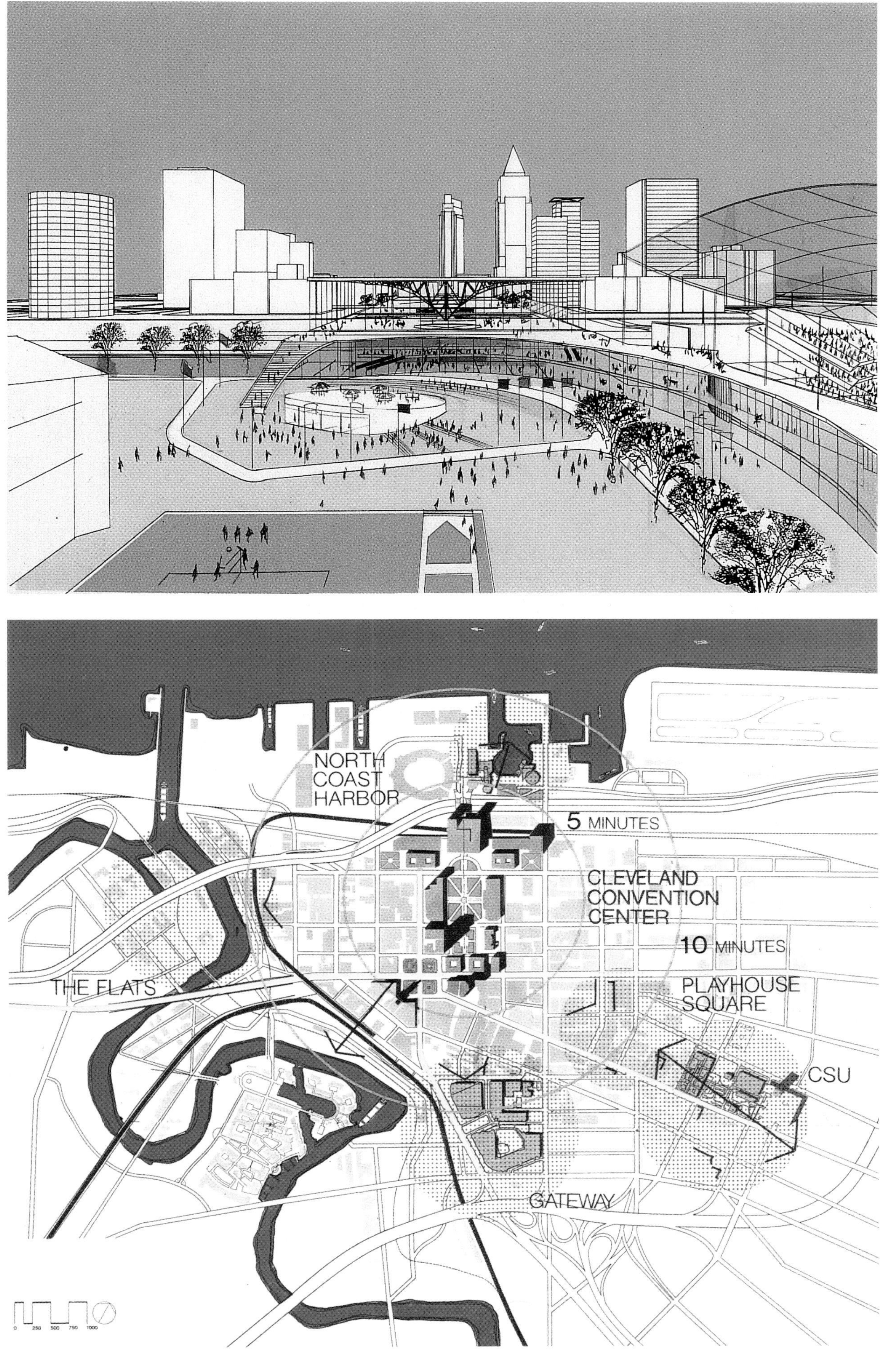

Volumetric plan of the project area and, below, overall site plan.

Top of page, central perspective view of the project and, bottom, a detail of the central zone.

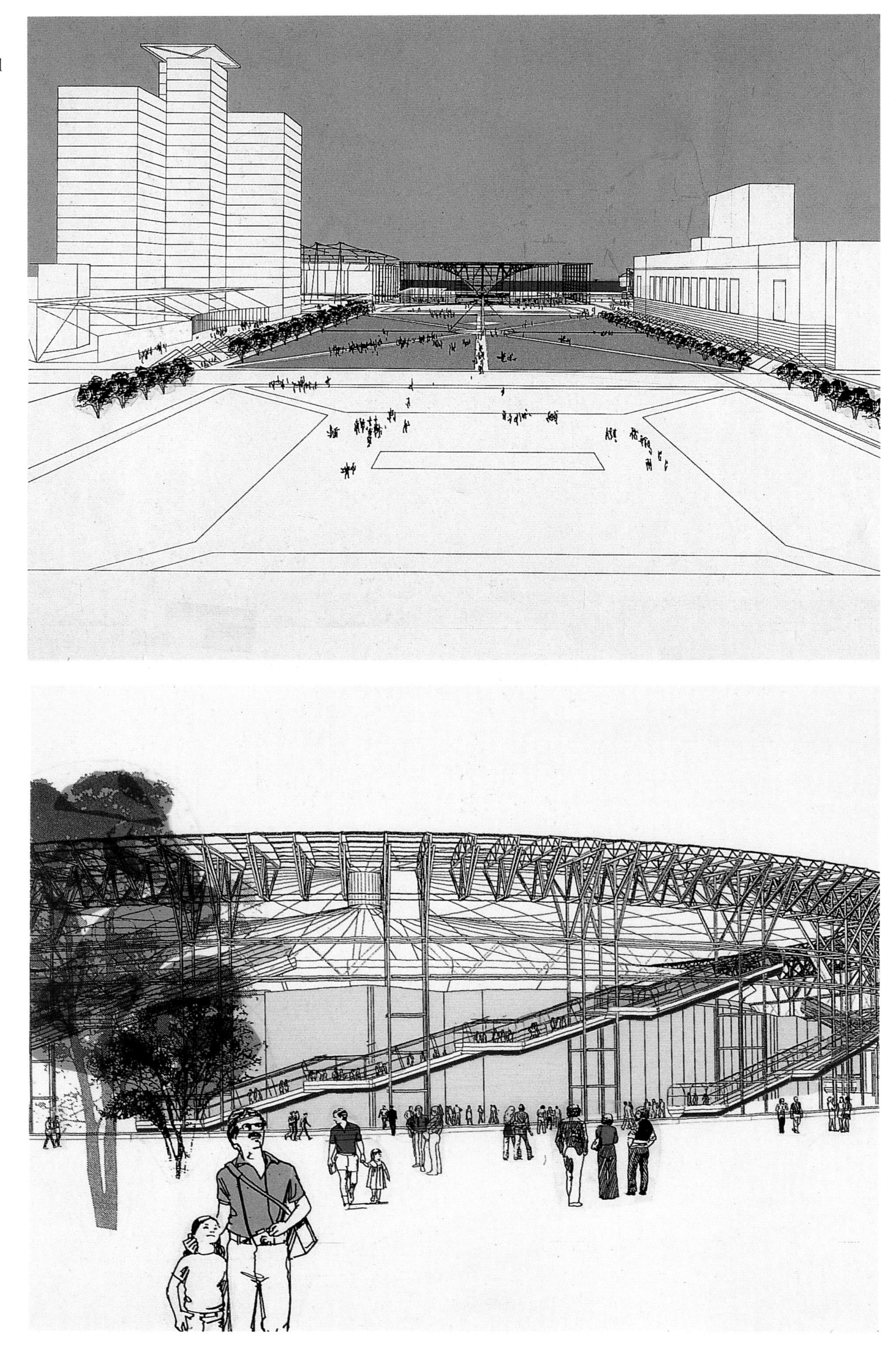

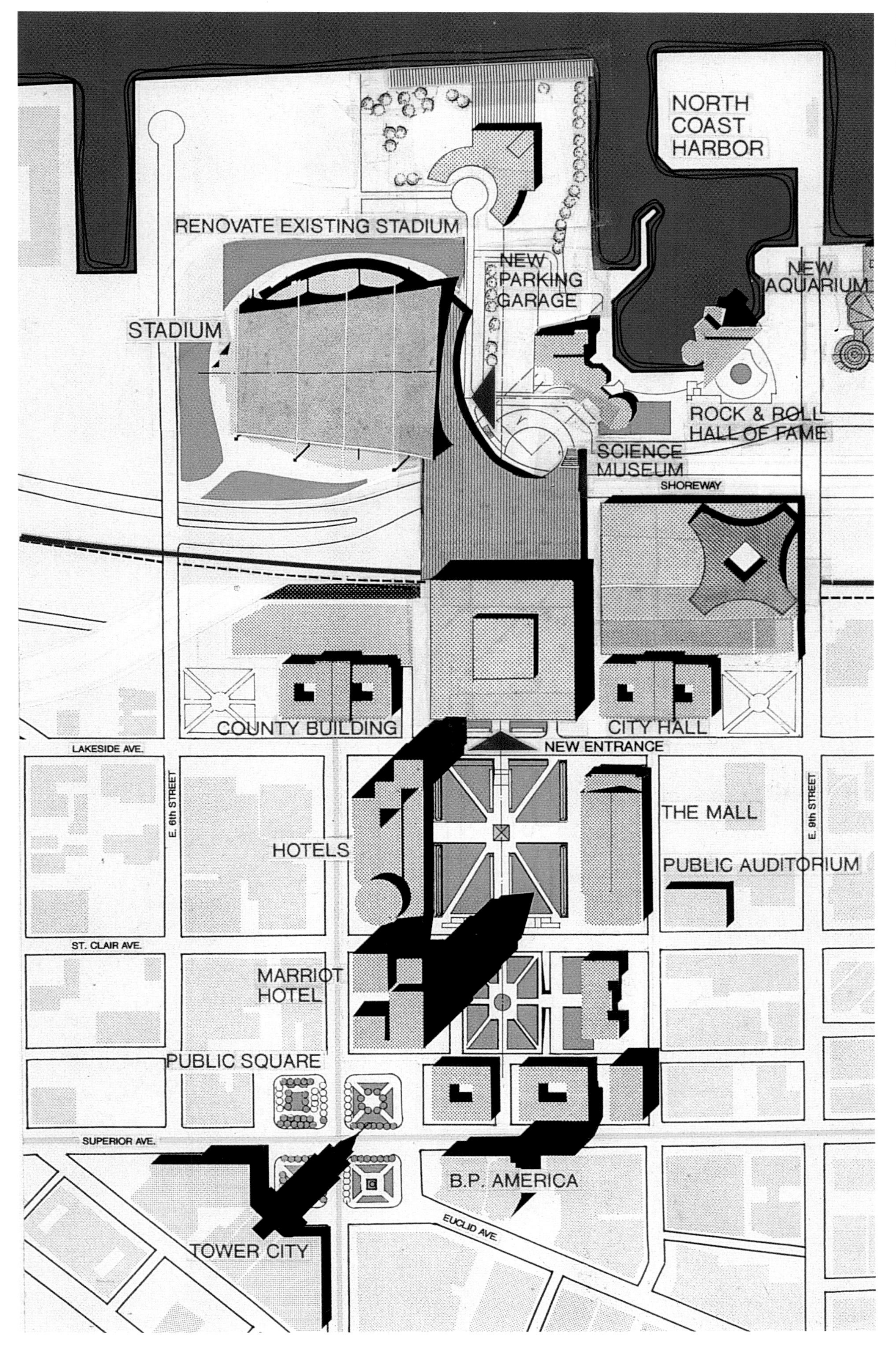

View of the model from the section overlooking the port.

Richard Fleischman Architects, Inc.

RICHARD FLEISCHMAN ARCHITECTS, INC.

Richard Fleischman Architects, Inc., founded in 1961, is a multi-faceted design and management firm of innovative professionals committed to excellence. It is organized to provide broad architectural and planning services, including research and programming, program management, feasibility/threshold studies, land use analysis, facilities evaluation, master planning, space planning, graphic and interior design. Its services also include cost estimating, value engineering, scheduling, competitive bidding and contract negotiation, coordination and observation of construction activities, and financial management of projects. Project types for the public and private sector include urban planning, commercial, retail, and residential developments, educational facilities (K-12 and higher education including campus planning), health-related and religious institutions, and performing and visual arts centers. Its professional services have been performed throughout the United States and abroad, as far a field as Michigan, Kansas, Oklahoma, Oregon, New York, Pennsylvania, Connecticut, West Virginia, Washington, Malawi, Africa, Guatemala, and Poland, Warsaw.

The spaces it creates reflect both its ideology and client's expectations. Facilities designed early on still have maintained their design integrity for the past three decades. Well designed spaces encourage and complement the functional and aesthetic process. Economic, political, and technological factors will continue to impact upon the future of the art of building and the perception of our environment. Its philosophy of planning and architecture is best described as dedication to the process of design. It believes the initial phase of planning permits the collaborative effort and freedom to participate completely and logically in the synthesis of final recommendations.

During the first three decades, the firm has completed more than three hundred projects. To sustain a high level of design and technical achievement, the capacities of the three partners are augmented by a staff of registered architects, designers, planners, graphic artists and administrative personnel. The firm is structured in a manner which keeps Richard Fleischman and partners in direct contact with each project through each phase of development. This control is evident in the consistent quality of the work produced, and ensures completion well ahead of schedule. Senior Partner, Richard Fleischman, FAIA, is ultimately responsible for design, while management and technological operations are the responsibility of partners Arthur Brenneman, AIA, and Clyde Horn, AIA. All nationally registered architects, each complements the other's design talents, technical expertise, and administrative skills. Richard Fleischman Architects believes that each client's project deserves the continuous personal service that a focused group of professionals can provide. This collaborative process has been extremely successful since the practice was founded in 1961.

For each project, the firm assembles a team of professionals, proven in their respective fields. It has been fortunate in forming a special alliance with world-renowned architects and engineers whose expertise brilliantly orchestrates significant structures throughout the world. Its consultant team is further complemented by specialists in all other disciplines who also have proven records of achievement. International periodicals (World Architecture, l'Arca, Architectural Record etc.) have recognized the achievements of this team's approach throughout the past three decades.

A successful project - whether it is planning, building, interior design, or renovation - is the result of close, intense collaboration between client and firm. This collaboration occurs at meetings, where challenge, as well as ultimate agreement at every stage of the process, lead to innovative, efficient designs fulfilling the client's goals.

The firm believes that a successful project requires a well-managed project plan and successful control of its execution. Its experience has shown that when project requirements are carefully defined and evaluated, planned and then controlled through monitoring, the proper results are obtained in the most timely and efficient manner.

Key Members

Richard Fleischman, FAIA, Senior Partner, maintains the overview of the entire project. His primary role is to constantly challenge the strategies and options identified to ensure that the most effective direction is adopted, satisfying all criteria and objectives economically, in a holistic manner. His participation in this aspect ranges from basic overall design concepts through a detailed development of all components. He also participates in strategy and progress meetings with each project, so that any issues or concerns that may arise may be dealt with in an expedient manner.
He has been responsible for the overall design of many commercial, retail and educational facilities. He is currently involved in the following: Gateway, Georgia State University, University of Toledo-College of Engineering, Tiffin University Library, Cleveland Public Library-Villa Angela Library and Cleveland City Hall.

Clyde Horn, AIA, provides the project management necessary to permit a fluid, timely completion of the project. He also provides the day-to-day management to guarantee a fully-integrated resolution to issues and concerns as they arise. Mr. Horn and Mr. Fleischman have worked on many projects together, specifically Kent State University, Gateway Underground Service facility, and others such as Beachwood High School Education Complex that includes a theater, gymnasium and indoor swimming pool.

Arthur Brenneman, AIA, Partner, provides organizational and analytical expertise, as he has on a variety of projects ranging from architectural works, such as office buildings, educational facilities, high technology centers, correctional facilities, and housing complexes, to master planning and urban planning studies. Mr. Brenneman and Mr. Fleischman have worked on many projects together, specifically, the Ohio Aerospace Institute, Project Architect for the award-winning Polymer Science Building for the University of Akron, Cleveland Public Library/Villa Angela complex, and master planning at Cleveland State University.

Chi Chen is responsible for computer development, and is currently expanding the firm's AutoCad activities to improve design strategies as well as construction documents. His background includes study in China and graduate work at Kent State University. Currently he is project manager for the Luke Easter recreational center and the Visitors' Bureau center for the Cleveland Bi-Centennial in 1996.

Awards and Honors

Award of Excellence 1995
Library Architecture
Cleveland Public Library
Lake Shore Facility
Cleveland, Ohio

Award-Best in Adaptive Reuse
Renovation 1995
InteriorsCleveland Public Library
Lake Shore Facility
Cleveland, Ohio

Award of Excellence 1994
Images, Australia
Cleveland Public Library
Breezy Bluff

Honor Award 1994
American Institute of Architects
Cleveland Chapter
Cleveland Public Library-LakeShore Facility
Cleveland, Ohio

Merit Award 1994
American Institute of Architects
Cleveland Chapter, Auburn Career Center
and Vocational School Facility,
Concord Township, Ohio

Global Recognition - MDO 1994
Outstanding Educational Facility
Ohio Aerospace Institute
Cleveland, Ohio

Award of Merit 1994
Renovation, Adaptive Reuse, IBD-CID
Cleveland Public Library
Memorial-Nottingham Branch
Cleveland, Ohio

Honorable Mention Award 1994
Public, Institutional, IBD-CID
Ohio Aerospace Institute
Cleveland, Ohio

Honor Award 1994
American Institute of Architects
Architects Society of Ohio
Cleveland Public Library
Memorial-Nottingham Branch
Cleveland, Ohio

Honorable Mention 1994-95
Northern Ohio LIVE
Cleveland Public Library
Memorial-Nottingham Branch Cleveland, Ohio

Citation Award 1994
National School Board Association
Eastlake High School
Seattle, Washington

Citation Award 1994
American Association of School Administrators
American Institute of Architects and
The Council of Educational Facility Planners
Int. Ohio Aerospace Institute
Brook Park, Ohio

Honor Award 1993
American Institute of Architects
Cleveland Chapter
Ohio Aerospace Institute
Brook Park, Ohio

Honor Award 1993
American Institute of Architects
Cleveland Chapter Utian Residence
Bratenahl, Ohio

Merit Award 1993
American Institute of Architects
Ohio Aerospace Institute
Brook Park, Ohio

Citation Award 1993
American School & Universities
Ohio Aerospace Institute
Brook Park,Ohio

Honor Award 1992
American Institute of Architects
Cleveland Chapter
Eugene Stevens Art Gallery
Cleveland, Ohio

Honor Award 1992
American Institute of Architects
Architects Society of Ohio
Polymer Science Building
Akron, Ohio

Award of Recognition 1992
Downtown Business Council
Greater Cleveland Growth Association
Cleveland, Ohio

Interior Design Award 1992
IBD, Cleveland Interior Design
Cleveland Center for Contemporary Art
Cleveland, Ohio

Interior Design Award 1992
IBD, Cleveland Interior Design
RFA Studios
1025 Huron Building
Cleveland, Ohio

Interior Design Award 1992
IBD, Cleveland Interior Design
County Human Services &
Support Agencies Building
Cleveland, Ohio

Honor Award 1991
American Institute of Architects
Cleveland Chapter
Polymer Science Building
The University of Akron, Akron, Ohio

Honor Award 1991
American Institute of Architects
Architects Society of Ohio
1025 Huron Building [RFA Studio]
Cleveland, Ohio

Award of Achievement in Architecture 1991-1992
Northern Ohio LIVE
Polymer Science Building
The University of Akron
Akron, Ohio

1991 Louis I. Kahn Award
American School & University
Polymer Science Building
The University of Akron
Akron, Ohio

Award of Design Excellence 1990 American Institute of Architects Cleveland Chapter Eugene Stevens Art Gallery
Cleveland, Ohio

Award of Design Excellence 1990
American Institute of Architects Cleveland Chapter Cleveland Center for Contemporary Art
Cleveland, Ohio

Award of Achievement in Architecture 1989-1990
Northern Ohio Live Champagne Edition
Cleveland Center for Contemporary Art
Cleveland, Ohio

Honor Award 1990
American Institute of Architects
Architects Society of Ohio
Cleveland Center for Contemporary Art
Cleveland, Ohio

Renovation Design Award 1990
Commercial Renovation, Adaptive Re-Use
Cleveland Center for Contemporary Art
Cleveland, Ohio

Honor Award 1989
American Institute of Architects
Architects Society of Ohio
Freestanding Alterations to General Mail Facility
Cleveland, Ohio

Gold Medal Firm Award 1988
American Institute of Architects
Architects Society of Ohio Most Distinguished Service to the Professional of Architecture

Award of Achievement in Architecture 1987-1988
Northern Ohio Live Champagne Edition
Stow-Munroe Falls High School
Stow, Ohio

Citation Award 1988
American Association of School Administrators
Stow-Munroe Falls High School
Stow, Ohio

Award of Design Excellence 1987
American Institute of Architects
Architects Society of Ohio
Stow-Munroe Falls High School
Stow, Ohio

Award of Merit 1987
Council of Educational Facility
Planners International
Stow-Munroe Falls High School
Stow, Ohio

Honor Award 1987
American Institute of Architects
Cleveland Chapter
Stow-Munroe Falls High School
Stow, Ohio

Honorable Mention 1987
American Institute of Architects
Cleveland Chapter
North Coast Harbor Development Master Plan
Cleveland, Ohio

Honorable Mention 1987
American Institute of Architects
Cleveland Chapter
Ashtabula High School Plan
Ashtabula, Ohio

Award of Design Excellence 1985
American Institute of Architects
Architects Society of Ohio Cox Cable, Cleveland
Parma, Ohio

Honorable Mention 1985
American Institute of Architects
Cleveland Chapter
Millersburg United Methodist Church
Millersburg, Ohio

Honorable Mention 1985
American Institute of Architects
Cleveland Chapter
Cox Cable Cleveland Area

Honor Award 1983
Architects Society of Ohio
American Institute of Architects
Viacom Communications
Cleveland Heights, Ohio

Award of Design Excellence 1983
American Institute of Architects
Cleveland Chapter Beachwood
Swimming Pool
Beachwood, Ohio

Award of Design Excellence 1982
American Institute of Architects Cleveland
Chapter Viacom Cablevision
Cleveland Heights, Ohio

Award of Superior 1982
American Economic Development Council
Downtown Cleveland Development Handbook

Award of Excellence 1982
Mid-America Economic Development County
Downtown Cleveland Development Handbook

Award of Design Excellence 1981
American Association of School Administrators
American Institute of Architects
Fremont Junior High School
Fremont, Ohio

Award of Design Excellence
and Energy Conservation 1981
National School Boards Association
American Institute of Architects
Fremont Junior High School
Fremont, Ohio

Award of Design Excellence 1981
American Association of School Administrators
American Institute of Architects
Beachwood High School Swimming Pool
Beachwood, Ohio

Merit Award
Innovative Design in Wood 1981
American Wood Council
Beachwood High School Swimming Pool
Beachwood, Ohio

Award of Design Excellence 1979
American Institute of Architects
Cleveland Chapter Automatic Data Processing
Cleveland, Ohio

Citation Award 1979
American Association
of School Administrators
Kent State University School of Physical
Education, Recreation and Dance
Kent, Ohio

Award of Design Excellence 1978
American Institute of Architects
Cleveland Chapter Beachwood High School
Physical Education Facility
Beachwood, Ohio

Award of Design Excellence 1978
American Institute of Architects
Cleveland Chapter Fairfax Elementary School
Cleveland, Ohio

Citation Award 1978
American Association of School Administrators
Goldwood Elementary School
Rocky River, Ohio

Citation Award 1978
American Association of School Administrators
Beachwood High School Physical Education
Beachwood, Ohio

Award of Design Excellence 1978
American Institute of Architects Cleveland
Chapter South Euclid Municipal Facility
South Euclid, Ohio

Merit Award 1977
Association of School Business Officials
Rocky River Board of Education
Administrative Center
Rocky River, Ohio

Citation Award 1977
American Association of School Administrators
Rocky River Junior High School
Rocky River, Ohio

Award of Excellence 1977
Association of School Business Officials
American Institute of Architects
Council of Educational Facilities Planners
Rocky River Board of Education
Rocky River, Ohio

Award of Excellence 1977
Association of School Business Officials
American Institute of Architects
Council of Educational Facilities Planners
Rocky River Junior High School
Rocky River, Ohio

Honor Award 1977
Architects Society of Ohio
Beachwood High School
Physical Education Facility
Beachwood, Ohio

Honor Award 1977
Architects Society of Ohio
Goldwood Elementary School
Rocky River, Ohio

Merit Award 1977
Architects Society of Ohio
Rocky River Board of Education
Administrative Center
Rocky River, Ohio

Merit Award 1977
Architects Society of Ohio
Fairfax Elementary School
Cleveland Heights, Ohio

Merit Award 1977
Architects Society of Ohio
Rocky River Junior High School
Rocky River, Ohio

Citation Award 1977
American Association
of School Administrators
Rocky River Junior High School
Rocky River, Ohio

Merit Award 1977
ASBO School Facilities Council
Rocky River Board of Education
Administrative Center
Rocky River, Ohio

Honor Award 1976
Guild for Religious Architecture
St. Paschal Baylon Church
Highland Heights, Ohio

Honor Award 1976
Architects Society of Ohio
Ashtabula Urban Redevelopment
Ashtabula, Ohio

Honor Award 1976
Architects Society of Ohio
Cleveland Skating Club
Shaker Heights, Ohio

Honor Award 1976
Architects Society of Ohio
Collens' Residence
Mesopotamia, Ohio

Honor Award 1976
Architects Society of Ohio
Our Lady of Perpetual Help Church
Aurora, Ohio

Honor Award 1975
Guild for Religious Architecture
Sacred Hearts Church
Mt. Gilead, Ohio

Merit Award 1975
Guild for Religious Architecture
Our Lady of Perpetual Help Church
Aurora, Ohio

Honor Award 1975
Architects Society of Ohio
South Euclid Service Facility
South Euclid, Ohio

Honor Award 1975
Architects Society of Ohio
Sacred Hearts Church
Mt. Gilead, Ohio

Award of Excellence 1975
Association of School Business Officials
American Institute of Architects
Council of Education Facility Planners
Cleveland Heights-University Heights Schools
(Design Coordinating Architect)

Design Award Citation 1974
Progressive Architecture
Cleveland Heights-University Heights School
(Design Coordinating Architect)

Walter Taylor Award 1974
American Association of School Administrators
Bellflower Elementary School
Mentor, Ohio

Award of Merit 1974
American Institute of Architects
Villa Angela Academy-Library
Cleveland, Ohio

Honor Award 1974
American Institute of Architects Ohio Region
Bayberry Landing, Lake Chautauqua, New York

Honor Award 1974
American Institute of Architects Ohio Region
Bellflower Elementary Mentor, Ohio

Honor Award 1974
American Institute of Architects Ohio Region
St. Paschal Baylon Church
Highland Heights, Ohio

Design Award Citation 1973
Progressive Architecture
Bellflower Elementary
Mentor, Ohio

Honor Award 1973
American Institute of Architects Ohio Region
Villa Angela Academy Cleveland, Ohio

Honor Award 1973
American Institute of Architects Ohio Region
Hallinan Center
Cleveland, Ohio

Certificate of Merit 1973
Greater Cleveland Growth Association
Villa Angela Academy Cleveland, Ohio

Certificate of Merit 1973
Greater Growth Association, Hallinan Center
Cleveland, Ohio

Honor Award 1972
Guild for Religious Architecture
Church of the Covenant
Cleveland, Ohio

Merit Award 1972
Greater Cleveland Growth Association
St. Paschal Baylon Church Highland Hts., Ohio

Honor Award 1971
American Institute of Architects Ohio Region
Church of the Covenant Cleveland, Ohio

Honor Award 1971
American Institute of Architects Ohio Region
Pioneer Memorial Church Solon, Ohio

Honor Award 1971
Guild for Religious Architecture
Chaminade Chapel
Karonga, Malawi, Africa

Honor Award 1971
American Institute of Architects
Ohio Region, St. Elizabeth Church
Columbus, Ohio

Certificate of Merit 1970
Greater Cleveland Growth
Association Church of the Covenant
Cleveland, Ohio

Liturgical Conference Award 1970
Liturgical Conference
Our Lady of Perpetual Help Church
Aurora, Ohio

Award of Merit 1969
National Catholic Educational Association
Catechetical Center, Warren, Michigan

Certificate of Merit 1969
Greater Cleveland Growth Association
Parma Heights Baptist Church
Parma Hts., Ohio

First Honor Award 1969
National Catholic Educational Association
St. Elizabeth Church
Columbus, Ohio

Award of Merit 1968
American Institute of Architects
Ohio Region
Bethel Lutheran Church
Middleburg Hts., Ohio

Honorable Mention 1966
Liturgical Conference
Holy Family Church and Convent
Parma, Ohio

Award of Merit 1966
American Institute of Architects Ohio Region
Church of St. Martin of Tours
Maple Heights, Ohio

Honorable Mention 1966
American Institute of Architects Ohio Region
Elyria District Catholic High School
Elyria, Ohio

First Honor Award 1965
American Institute of Architects Ohio Region
Orrville Methodist Church
Orrville, Ohio

Lecaro Gold Medal 1965
Liturgical Conference
St. Jude Church and Convent
Warrensville Hts., Ohio

Honorable Mention 1965
Liturgical Conference
Our Lady Queen of Peach of Church
Harper Woods, Michigan

Award of Merit 1964
Prestressed Concrete Association
St. Eugene Church
Bedford, Ohio

Award of Merit 1964
Prestressed Concrete Association
Rockport Methodist Church
Rocky River, Ohio